THE MARINER'S BOOK of DAYS

PETER H. SPECTRE

Thanks to Jonathan Wilson, Lindy Gifford, Sherry Streeter, Jane Crosen, Kathleen Brandes, and the staff at WoodenBoat Books for their fine efforts on the production of this book.

© 2002 by Peter H. Spectre
Compass Rose, 4 Patten Point Road, Spruce Head, Maine 04859

All rights reserved. No part of the contents of this calendar may be reproduced in any form without the written consent of the publisher. All inquiries should be directed to: The Editor, WoodenBoat Books, P.O. Box 78, Brooklin, ME 04616.

Design by Sherry Streeter and Lindy Gifford

Printed in China

Cover: "Lost in the Fog," oil painting by William Edward Norton (1843–1916). From the collection of The William A. Farnsworth Library and Art Museum. For further information, write the Museum at P.O. Box 466, Rockland, Maine 04841, or visit www.farnsworthmuseum.org.

A WoodenBoat Book
www.woodenboat.com

ISBN 0-937822-70-1

At last we hoisted the stun'-sails up to the top-sail yards, and as soon as the vessel felt them she gave a sort of bound like a horse, and the breeze blowing more and more, she went plunging along, shaking off the foam from her bows like foam from a bridle-bit. Every mast and timber seemed to have a pulse in it that was beating with life and joy, and I felt a wild exulting in my own heart, and felt as if I would be glad to bound along so round the world.

—from *Redburn*, by Herman Melville

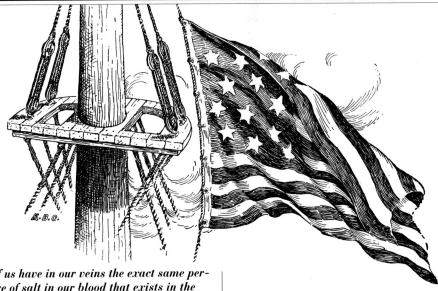

All of us have in our veins the exact same percentage of salt in our blood that exists in the ocean, and, therefore, we have salt in our blood, in our sweat, in our tears. We are tied to the ocean. And when we go back to the sea, whether it is to sail or to watch it, we are going back from whence we came. —John F. Kennedy

What is there in the universe more fascinating than running water and the possibility of moving over it? What better image of existence and possible triumph. —George Santayana

I find the great thing in this world is not so much where we stand, as in what direction we are moving—we must sail sometimes with the wind and sometimes against it—but we must sail, and not drift, nor lie at anchor. —Oliver Wendell Holmes

UNDERWAY, FLY THE U.S. ENSIGN
- Powerboat—if equipped with a mast and gaff, from the gaff; otherwise from the stern staff.
- Sportfisherman—if a stern staff will be in the way of the action, from a halyard rigged behind the tower.
- Sailboat, low-aspect-ratio marconi rig—from the leech of the aftermost sail, two-thirds of the way up from the clew.
- Sailboat, high-aspect-ratio marconi rig—from the stern staff.
- Sailboat, gaff rig—from the peak of the aftermost gaff.
- All sailboats under power alone—from the stern staff.

THE YACHT *LIVELY SALLY*, OFF MALAGA, SPAIN, NEW YEAR'S DAY, 1882

Having rejoiced over two yachts which have come into Gibraltar crippled (one of them twenty days from Cowes with her bulwarks washed away) while we have not carried away a rope-yarn; having dined with Charley from Aldershot, filled up with water, and laid in a sack of new potatoes and some fresh meat, we got under way yesterday, bound for Algiers. We started with a little air from the westward but it is needless to say that we were hardly clear of Europe Point before it first fell calm and then began to blow from E.N.E., which is as nearly dead on end as a Mediterranean wind can manage. We have, therefore, done but little good, and this evening as I write, there is a big ring round the moon, the wind is singing a lively little tune among the rigging, and the little vessel is beginning to jump in a way which makes us foresee that we shall come badly off for dinner.
—Thomas Gibson Bowles

UNDERWAY IN FOREIGN WATERS, AS A COURTESY FLY THE FLAG OF THE COUNTRY OF JURISDICTION
- Powerboat with no mast—from the bow staff.
- Powerboat with mast and spreaders—from the starboard spreader; if two masts, from the forward starboard spreader.
- Sailboat—from the starboard spreader; if two masts, from the forward starboard spreader.
- Continue to fly the U.S. ensign in the customary manner.

To be on water is a comfort to the soul of man.
—Carleton Mitchel

DEC/JAN

Monday
30

1941—The SS *Patrick Henry*, the first ship of the Liberty type, entered service.

Tuesday
31 NEW YEAR'S EVE

1964—*Bluebird K7*, driven by Donald Campbell, set a world jet-powered water speed record of 276.3 mph on Lake Dumbleyung, Australia.

Wednesday
1 NEW YEAR'S DAY

1878—The first annual edition of *Lloyd's Register of Yachts* was published in Britain.

Thursday
2

1932—The first frostbite race, for sailing dinghies, got underway on Manhasset Bay, Port Washington, New York.

Friday
3

1854—The record-setting clipper ship *Lightning*, designed and built by Donald McKay, was launched in East Boston, Massachusetts.

Saturday
4

1910—The USS *Michigan*, the first U.S. battleship of the Dreadnought type, was commissioned.

Sunday
5

1779—Stephen Decatur, hero of the U.S. Navy, was born at Sunnepuxent, Maryland.

THE SNEAKBOX *CENTENNIAL REPUBLIC*, MISSISSIPPI RIVER NEAR SKIPWITH LANDING, MISSISSIPPI, JANUARY 12, 1876

My sleep had been much broken by night-travelling, and about nine o'clock on Wednesday evening I fastened my boat to the flat [raft], and determined to have two or three hours of refreshing slumber. An hour's peaceful rest followed, and then a snorting, screeching stern-wheel steamer crossed the river with its tow of barges, and demoralized all my surroundings, driving me against the flat, and shooting water over the deck of my craft. Only half awake, I cast off from the flat, and thought that I was rowing down-river as usual; but I had dropped back into my nest just for one moment, and was in the land of Nod.

—Nathaniel H. Bishop

If you are going to buy a boat, either the first or last one, make up your mind thoroughly as to what kind of a craft you want, and what you want her for. —Thomas Fleming Day

For my choice I revel in a warmly lighted cabin where three or four can recline with feet up at day's end. —Maurice Griffiths

COMFORTABLE CRUISING ACCOMMODATIONS
- Uncomplicated cabin layout
- Provision for privacy, even if only temporary screening
- Enclosed head, with room for the average person to turn around
- Ventilation, and plenty of it
- Screening against insects
- Both natural and artificial light, placed where it is needed
- Standing headroom in the galley
- Guardrail on the galley stove
- Large, easily accessible icebox with proper drain
- Solid-fuel heating stove if cruising in cold climates
- Flat surface for charts
- Wet locker for foulweather gear
- Tight deck
- Permanent bunk of adequate size for each member of the crew

MINIMUM DIMENSIONS OF A LARGE MAN'S BERTH, ACCORDING TO IAN NICOLSON
Length—6 feet, 4 inches
Width at shoulders and hips—1 foot, 9 inches
Width at foot—1 foot, 1 inch
Width at head—1 foot, 4 inches

*The Owl and the Pussy-Cat went to sea
In a beautiful pea-green boat.*
—Edward Lear

JANUARY

Monday
6

1839—A savage two-day winter gale hit the port of Liverpool, England, sinking several vessels with much loss of life and driving the N.W. Lightship from her moorings.

Tuesday
7

1947—The U.S. icebreaker *Northwind*, the rescue submarine *Stennet*, and the supply ships *Yance* and *Merrick* became stuck in an ice floe near the Antarctic Circle.

Wednesday
8

1609—Henry Hudson signed a contract with the *Verenigde Oostindische Compagnie*—the Dutch East India Company—to undertake a voyage to the westward to seek a northern route to the East Indies.

Thursday
9

1918—The U.S. Naval Overseas Transportation Service, the mission of which was to carry essential cargo for U.S. military operations during World War I, was established.

Friday
10

1892—The extreme clipper ship *N.B. Palmer*, one of the last of her type still afloat, was abandoned in the North Atlantic east of the Grand Bank.

Saturday
11

1757—Alexander Hamilton, the father of the Treasury Department's Revenue-Cutter Service, the forerunner of the U.S. Coast Guard, was born.

Sunday
12

1923—The title "Commandant" was authorized for the chief commanding officer of the U.S. Coast Guard.

IN THE EVENT YOU WERE THINKING THAT KNOWLEDGE OF SEA CHANTIES WAS DEAD AND GONE—A BIBLIOGRAPHY

The Early Naval Ballads of England, by J.O. Halliwell, Cambridge, England, 1841
Naval Songs, by S.B. Luce, New York, 1883
The Music of the Waters, by Laura A. Smith, London, 1888
Songs of Sea and Sail, by Thomas Fleming Day, New York, 1898
Old Sea Chanties, by J. Bradford and A. Fagge, London, 1904
Sailors' Songs or Chanties, by Ferris Tozer and F.J. Davis, London, 1906
Sea Songs and Shanties, by Captain W.B. Whall, 1910
Shanties and Forebitters, by Mrs. Clifford Beckett, London, 1914
Songs of Sea Labour, by Frank T. Bullen and W.F. Arnold, London, 1915
King's Book of Chanties, by Stanton H. King, Boston & New York, 1918
Capstan Chanteys, by Cecil K. Sharp, London, 1919
Pulling Chanteys, by Cecil K. Sharp, London, 1919
Deep Sea Chanties, by Owen Trevine, London, 1921
The Shanty Book, Part I, by R.R. Terry, London, 1921
Sea Songs and Ballads, C. Fox Smith, London, 1923
Roll and Go: Songs of American Sailormen, by Joanna C. Colcord, Indianapolis, 1924
Sea Chanties, by Geoffrey Toye, London, 1924
Songs of the Sea and Sailors' Chanteys, by Robert Frothingham, Boston, 1924
Ballads and Songs of the Shanty-Boy, by Franz L. Rickaby, Boston, 1926
The Shanty Book, Part II, by R.R. Terry, London, 1926
The Seven Seas Shanty Book, by John Sampson, London, 1927
A Book of Shanties, by C. Fox Smith, London, 1927
Salt Sea Ballads, by R.R. Terry, London, 1931
American Sea Songs and Chanteys, by Frank Shay, New York, 1948
Shantymen and Shantyboys: Songs of the Sailor and the Lumbermen, by W.M. Doerflinger, New York, 1951
The Shell Book of Shanties, London, 1952
Sea Songs of Sailing, Whaling and Fishing, by Burl Ives, New York, 1956
Shanties from the Seven Seas: Shipboard Work-Songs from the Great Days of Sail, by Stan Hugill, London, 1961
Sailor's Songs and Shanties, by Michael Hurd, London, 1965
Shanties and Sailors' Songs, by Stan Hugill, London, 1969

THE BARK *LORTON*, FIRTH OF CLYDE, SCOTLAND, JANUARY 13, 1913

The tug arrived and we manned the capstan to heave up the anchor for the last time. As we trudged round, pushing on the capstan bars, we sang the old sea shanties now reserved for stage and studio. With the fifteen fathom shackle in sight, Sails (our sailmaker) started the "Farewell Shanty," one that described so well that end-of-the-voyage feeling of the old sailing ship sailors.

Solo: I thought I heard the "Old Man" say,
Chorus: Leave her, Johnnie, leave her!
Solo: To-morrow you will get your pay,
Chorus: It's time for us to leave her....

We towed across the Firth of Clyde to Ardrossan Docks; then made the *Lorton* fast alongside the quay. "That'll do, men!" With those words the Mate dismissed the crew.

—A.G. Course

The idea of escaping the problems of life by sailing away is a fable.
—Tristan Jones

JANUARY

Monday
13

1813—A squadron of Britain's Royal Navy began a blockade of the Chesapeake and Delaware Bays.

Tuesday
14

1920—The five-masted schooner *Fenix*, formerly the *Helen W. Martin*, the largest schooner-rigged vessel ever registered in Sweden, went ashore on the coast of Denmark and was lost.

Wednesday
15

1898—Uffa Fox, sailor, yacht designer, author, bon vivant, was born in East Cowes, Isle of Wight, England.

Thursday
16

1930—The aircraft carrier USS *Lexington* provided electrical power to the city of Tacoma, Washington, when floods disabled the city's power plants.

Friday
17

1832—The use of naval officers to command vessels of the Revenue-Marine, predecessor of the U.S. Coast Guard, was discontinued; future vacancies would come from promotion within the service.

Saturday
18

1812—The *Comet*, the first passenger steamboat built in Europe, achieved 7½ knots on the River Clyde, Scotland.

Sunday
19

1988—Most members of the U.S. Merchant Marine who served in World War II were given veteran status by the U.S. government.

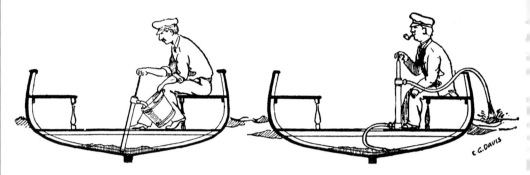

PUMP THAT BILGE

Small craft at the very least should have a scoop bailer, or a portable hand pump with a hose long enough to reach over the side; preferably both.

Larger craft should have redundant systems: fixed hand pump, fixed power pump, portable hand pump, and buckets suitable for bailing. DO NOT depend on a power pump alone. In an emergency, bail water into the head and then pump it out. In a real emergency, use the engine's cooling water pump as a bilge pump by removing the seawater intake hose from the hull fitting and running it into the bilge.

When the porpoise jumps,
Look out for your pumps.
                —old weather saying

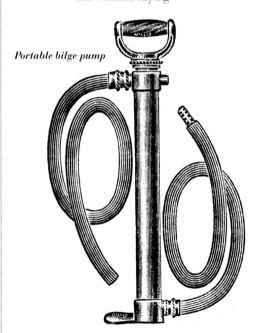

Portable bilge pump

HOW TO TELL WHETHER A LEAK IS INCREASING

With a hand pump, pump the bilge at regular intervals—every hour, day, week, etc., as necessary.

Count how many strokes it takes to empty the bilge.

If the number of strokes increases per interval, the leak is increasing; the difference in strokes will tell you the rate of increase.

IT IS GOOD WHEN IT STINKETH

When a ship is staunch, that is takes in but little water into her hold, she is said to be tight. And this tightness is best known by the very smell of the water that is pumped out of her; for when it stinketh much, it is a sign that the water hath lain long in the hold of the ship; and on the contrary, when it is clear and sweet, it is a token that it comes freshly in from the sea. This stinking water therefore is always a welcome perfume to an old seaman; and he that stops his nose at it is laughed at, and held but a fresh-water man at best.
                —from *Boteler's Dialogues*, 1634

THE SHIP *WALPOLE*, NORTH ATLANTIC, WITH A CARGO OF WHEAT, JANUARY 22, 1847

Heavy gales from N.W. and rough sea. Squalls, snow and hail.... Trying pumps but could not get any water from them, the ship laying down so much upon her broad side the water would not come to them at all. Tried the bilge pumps, but they would not work—soon choked with wheat—at 12 midnight sounded the pumps; found two feet water in the well room; pumped a few strokes and the boxes became choked.
                —Captain Josiah Richardson

He who goes to sea for pleasure would go to hell for a pastime.
—Samuel Johnson

JANUARY

Monday
20
MARTIN LUTHER KING DAY

1914—The sailing ship *Inverclyde*, on a voyage from Seattle to Queenstown, Ireland, was knocked down and stayed down; three days later, after pumping and restowing cargo, the crew got her upright and sailing again.

Tuesday
21

1882—Rockwell Kent, artist, author of *N by E* and *Voyaging*, was born in Westchester, New York.

Wednesday
22

To sail uncharted waters and follow virgin shores—
what a life for men!   —Rockwell Kent

Thursday
23

1946—Lieutenant Commander Joseph T. O'Callahan became the first chaplain in the U.S. Navy to be awarded the Congressional Medal of Honor.

Friday
24

1884—John Alden, yacht designer, best known for his schooners derived from working vessels, was born in Troy, New York.

Saturday
25
BURNS NIGHT / UK & SCOTLAND

1799—Reference was first made in congressional legislation to "revenue cutters," the forerunners of present-day Coast Guard cutters.

Sunday
26

1983—A storm battered the coast of California, causing record high tides, surf over 30 feet, and much coastal damage.

WHEN BUYING A BOAT, TAKE YOUR TIME

Examine it thoroughly.

Seek advice, check out the source of the advice, look into the history of the boat, ask around.

Do not succumb to the heat of the moment.

Do not surrender to pressure from the seller. Especially do not fall for the classic story that there's another buyer getting ready to write a check.

Keep in mind that the buyer has the upper hand, and do not allow the seller to convince you otherwise.

Make your offer contingent on a satisfactory survey and on financing, if necessary, and put it in writing.

Do not allow the seller to select the surveyor.

Do not accept the results of a previous survey; that is, one commissioned by the seller or a buyer who subsequently backed out.

If the boat is in the water, have the boat hauled and surveyed out of the water.

In your written offer, make clear that any deposit must be returned if the survey is not satisfactory, and that you, the buyer, will be the final judge of what constitutes "satisfactory."

WHAT TYPE OF BOAT SHOULD I HAVE? DON'T ASK ME, SAYS MAURICE GRIFFITHS

There is, needless to say, no simple answer to this one, for selecting the most suitable boat for someone else is no easier than choosing him the best car, the best house, or the best job. It is very much a matter of opinion and of personal preferences.

THE MOST BASIC CONSIDERATIONS, ACCORDING TO A. HYATT VERRILL

The three most important matters to be considered in any boat are seaworthiness, stability, and speed. Which of these is of the greatest importance varies largely upon the local conditions, the purposes for which the boat is to be used, and the ideas of its builder or owner.

As a general rule, the most seaworthy boats are the most stable, while usually both stability and seaworthiness must be sacrificed to a certain degree in order to obtain great speed.

THE CLIPPER SHIP *ANDREW JACKSON*, SOUTH ATLANTIC OCEAN, SOUTHEAST OF MONTEVIDEO, FEBRUARY 1, 1860

Wednsday, Lat. 38.49, Lon. 53.06, NE, North, NW to WNW, First part Light Middle part Modrat Breeze and plesant Latter part Modrat the Sea has gon Down and the water is Light Colour this is Remarkable weather for these lattetude Strong Curent to the South S East (We have had a Strong Curent to Day it Must have benn from the River [the Río de la Plata—River Plate]).

—Captain J.E. Williams

Sometimes for brief periods it's kind of fun to make believe that you don't own a boat.
—Joe Richards

JAN/FEB

Monday
27
1900—In a three-hour struggle, a pulling-boat crew from the Whitehead (Maine) Life-Saving Station succeeded in towing with oars alone the becalmed schooner *Nelson Y. McFarland* from near-destruction on ledges to the safety of Seal Harbor.

Tuesday
28
1859—The shipyard of W.H. Brown, New York City, launched three paddlewheel steamers within an hour and a half of each other.

Wednesday
29
1946—The Nova Scotia racing-fishing schooner *Bluenose* struck a reef off the port of Aux Cayes, Haiti, and sank.

Thursday
30
1975—The wreck of the USS *Monitor*, the Civil War ironclad, sunk in a gale off Cape Hatteras in 1862, was declared the first U.S. underwater marine sanctuary.

Friday
31
1961—Lieutenant Commander Samuel Lee Gravely, Jr., became the first African-American to command a combat ship of the U.S. Navy, the USS *Falgout*.

Saturday
1
CHINESE NEW YEAR (YEAR OF THE GOAT)

Sunday
2
GROUNDHOG DAY

ONE WAY TO SUMMON THE WIND

The kitten at last recovered, to the great joy of the good captain: but to the great disappointment of some of the sailors, who asserted that the drowning of a cat was the very surest way of raising a favourable wind.

—Henry Fielding

EXPECT WIND IF ANY OF THESE EXIST
- Clouds with bright edges
- Rainbows
- Unusually clear atmosphere

FROM *THE RIME OF THE ANCIENT MARINER*

But soon there breathed a wind on me,
Nor sound nor motion made:
Its path was not upon the sea,
In ripple or in shade.

It raised my hair, it fanned my cheek
Like a meadow-gale of spring—
It mingled strangely with my fears,
Yet it felt like a welcoming.

Swiftly, swiftly flew the ship,
Yet she sailed softly too:
Sweetly, sweetly blew the breeze—
On me alone it blew.

—Samuel Taylor Coleridge

THE WHALESHIP *GIPSY*, IN THE DOLDRUMS, ATLANTIC OCEAN, FEBRUARY 4, 1843

Calm: fine & excessively sultry: Therm: at 85 degrees: you can form no idea of the state of people's feelings on board a ship, so long out as this, all anxious to get to the journey's end; yet, day after day hung in the "doldrums," yet trying to shove her along by bracing the yards to every breath of wind or cat's paws, that promise something of a breeze but die away ere they reach the ship, & thus amount to nothing: Portuguese men-of-war or Medusa are seen floating on the smooth sea, with expanded sail in form of the segment of a circle, clear, shining & of a pink colour, its rounded & upper edge being fringed: numerous tentaculae depended into the water: they possess a stinging or venomous property: small fish swam beneath.

—John Wilson

ON THE NORTHEAST COAST OF THE UNITED STATES

North winds send hail,
South winds bring rain.
East winds we bewail,
West winds blow amain.
Northeast is too cold,
Southeast not too warm.
Northwest is too bold,
Southwest blows no harm.

—anon.

COASTAL BREEZES

During the day—sea breeze, caused by air becoming heated over the land and rising, thus drawing cool air in from the sea. At night—land breeze, caused by air becoming cooled over the land and falling, resulting in an outflow of air toward the sea.

Sailors get sentimental when the trade winds blow.
—Arthur Mason

FEBRUARY

Monday
3

1796—*The American Coast Pilot* by Captain Lawrence Furlong, the first U.S.-originated book of sailing directions—Passamaquoddy Bay to the Virginia Capes—was published in Newburyport, Massachusetts.

Tuesday
4

1889—The French company undertaking to build a ship canal across the Isthmus of Panama declared bankruptcy.

Wednesday
5

1925—Naval aviator Lieutenant H.J. Brow made the first night landing on the U.S. Navy's first aircraft carrier, the USS *Langley*.

Thursday
6

1978—"The Fo'castle," naturalist and writer Henry Beston's "Outermost House" on Nauset Beach, Cape Cod, was blown from the top of a dune into the sea during a great storm that swept New England's coast, causing extreme destruction and severe coastal flooding.

Friday
7

1905—A 60-foot ocean wave, preceding cyclone winds of 120 mph, struck the South Pacific island of Tahiti, inundating Papeete, destroying nearby Tarona, and driving several vessels high onto the shore.

Saturday
8

1921—Colin Archer, designer of *redningsskoites* (rescue ships) and other seaworthy craft, died in Larvik, Norway.

Sunday
9

1870—The U.S. Congress authorized the Secretary of War to establish a Weather Bureau.

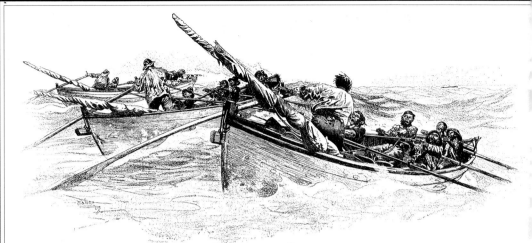

TEN GREAT NOVELS OF THE SEA
Moby-Dick, by Herman Melville
The Old Man and the Sea, by Ernest Hemingway
Captains Courageous, by Rudyard Kipling
Bird of Dawning, by John Masefield
The Wreck of the Grosvenor, by W. Clark Russell
Lord Jim, by Joseph Conrad
The Distant Shore, by Jan de Hartog
Delilah, by Marcus Goodrich
Treasure Island, by Robert Louis Stevenson
Gallions Reach, by H.M. Tomlinson

TEN TRASHY—BUT ENTERTAINING—NOVELS OF THE SEA
Captain Blood, by Rafael Sabatini
H.M.S. Ulysses, by Alistair MacLean
The Wreck of the Mary Deare, by Hammond Innes
A Prayer for the Ship, by Douglas Reeman
Mister Roberts, by Thomas Heggin
Submerged, by Edward Ellsberg
Call of the Offshore Wind, by Ralph Paine
Blood Knot, by Sam Llewellyn
The Hunt for Red October, by Tom Clancy
Voyage, by Sterling Hayden

THE NEW BEDFORD WHALESHIP *ROMAN*, AT SEA, FEBRUARY 10, 1871

It is quite rough today. But is a fair wind. We have 135 barrels of oil, 60 of hump back and 75 of sperm. We had two birds, there is one now. One died. There names were Dick and Lulu. Dick died. Lulu is going to.
 Good Bye for To Day
—Laura Jernegan, age nine

Outside of a dog, a book is a man's best friend. Inside of a dog, it's too dark to read.
—Groucho Marx

A BIG NOVEL REQUIRES A BIG SUBJECT

One often hears of writers that rise and swell with their subject, though it may seem but an ordinary one. How, then, with me, writing of this Leviathan? Unconsciously my chirography expands into placard capitals. Give me a condor's quill! Give me Vesuvius' crater for an inkstand! Friends, hold my arms! For in the mere act of penning my thoughts of this Leviathan, they weary me, and make me faint with their outreaching comprehensiveness of sweep, as if to include the whole circle of the sciences, and all the generations of whales, and men, and mastodons, past, present, and to come, with all the revolving panoramas of empire on earth, and throughout the whole universe, not excluding its suburbs. Such, and so magnifying, is the virtue of a large and liberal theme! We expand to its bulk. To produce a mighty book, you must choose a mighty theme. No great and enduring volume can ever be written on the flea, though many there be who have tried it.

—Herman Melville, *Moby-Dick*

The sailor is well aware that the stalls are filled with sea books written by landlubbers.
—Lincoln Colcord

FEBRUARY

Monday
10

1844—The steam-powered paddle-wheel sloop *Janus*—identical at each end, with rudders fore and aft, figureheads bow and stern, and able to reverse course without turning—was launched in Chatham, England.

Tuesday
11

1971—The United States and the Soviet Union signed a treaty prohibiting the deployment of nuclear weapons on the floor of the ocean.

Wednesday
12 LINCOLN'S BIRTHDAY

1907—The steamer *Larchmont* sank in Long Island Sound, New York; 131 people died.

Thursday
13

1950—Rafael Sabatini, author of *Captain Blood*, *The Sea Hawk*, and other romantic novels of the sea, died in Adelboden, Switzerland.

Friday
14 VALENTINE'S DAY

1779—Captain James Cook, Royal Navy, the great navigator, was murdered by natives at Kealakekua Bay, Sandwich Islands (Hawaii).

Saturday
15

1743—Joseph Banks, explorer and naturalist, circumnavigator of the globe with Captain Cook, was born in London, England.

Sunday ○
16

1926—The U.S. Congress authorized construction of the United States Coast Guard Academy, New London, Connecticut.

POLAR ICE

Ice, mostly in the polar regions, covers approximately 10 percent of the Earth's surface.

There is as much ice in Antarctica as there is water in the Atlantic Ocean.

The sea level would rise more than 500 feet if all the ice in the polar regions should melt.

More icebergs originate in the Arctic Ocean than the Antarctic.

THE AWE-INSPIRING ICEBERG, ACCORDING TO RICHARD HENRY DANA

No pencil has ever yet given anything like the true effect of an iceberg. In a picture they are huge, uncouth masses, stuck in the sea, while their chief beauty and grandeur—their slow, stately motion, the whirling of the snow about their summits, and the fearful groaning and cracking of their parts—the picture cannot give.

THE RESEARCH BARK *SCOTIA*, NEAR CAPE ADARE, ANTARCTICA, FEBRUARY 23, 1903

Soon after 5 a.m., having lain since midnight, we started steaming again through bay-ice, newly formed, of about five inches in thickness, every here and there crossing streams of ice about one year old, running transversely across our bows, and firmly fixed by that newly formed. Only at rare intervals was there a little lane of water. The ship headed north–northeast towards a berg which was sighted at midnight. It was beautiful to see the *Scotia* cutting through this ice, which is already very tough. As a rule a long split was produced right ahead of her, through which she was able to forge ahead. The more completely formed white ice seemed to be easier for her than the thinner black which is more gluey in texture and less brittle.

—William Speirs Bruce

ICEBERG CLASSIFICATIONS

	Height	Length
Growler	less than 3 feet	less than 16 feet
Bergy bit	3 to 13 feet	16 to 46 feet
Small	14 to 50 feet	47 to 200 feet
Medium	51 to 150 feet	201 to 400 feet
Large	151 to 240 feet	401 to 670 feet
Very large	over 240 feet	over 670 feet

TRANSATLANTIC LINERS KNOWN OR THOUGHT TO HAVE BEEN SUNK BY ICEBERGS

City of Glasgow, 1854 *City of Limerick*, 1881
Tempest, 1857 *Erin*, 1889
United Kingdom, 1868 *Naronic*, 1893
City of Boston, 1870 *Titanic*, 1912

TRANSATLANTIC LINERS THAT STRUCK ICEBERGS AND SURVIVED

Arizona, 1879
Gascoigne, 1897 (trapped in an ice field for days)
City of Rome, 1899

*Who shall put forth on thee,
Unfathomable Sea?*
—Percy Bysshe Shelley

FEBRUARY

Monday
17 PRESIDENT'S DAY

1755—Thomas Truxton, one of the first six captains commissioned in the U.S. Navy and first commander of the frigate *Constellation*, was born on Long Island, New York.

Tuesday
18

1952—Two tankers of the T-2 type, the *Fort Mercer* and the *Pendleton*, broke in half off the coast of New England during a severe northeast storm.

Wednesday
19

1904—The square-rigger *Henry B. Hyde*, considered to have been the most beautiful of the Down-Easter type ever built, went ashore near Cape Henry, Virginia, and became a total loss.

Thursday
20

1805—Navigation reopened on the Potomac River after having been blocked by ice for two months.

Friday
21

1688—The first written reference to Lloyd's Coffee House, the informal center of the maritime insurance business in London, England, later Lloyd's of London, was published in the *London Gazette*.

Saturday
22 WASHINGTON'S BIRTHDAY

Sunday
23

1882—Anton Otto Fischer, noted for his illustrations of ships and the sea in the *Saturday Evening Post*, was born in Munich, Germany.

THE CLIPPER *LIGHTNING* AT THE TIME OF HER LAUNCHING, ACCORDING TO A CONTEMPORARY DESCRIPTION IN *THE BOSTON DAILY ATLAS*

The run is very long and clean, but is much fuller than the bow, and under the stern it is rounded, so that it has no hollow counter for the sea to strike against when the ship settles aft. Her after motions, therefore, will be easy in a heavy sea, and when she is going at her highest speed, the after vacuum in the water will be filled by the run, so as to enable her to sail upon the same lines forward and aft. It is well known that ships with hollow counters, when in a heavy sea, bring up aft with a tremendous splash, that makes everything crack fore and aft, and that when going swiftly through the water, they settle down almost to the taffrails. The *Lightning*'s afterbody was designed with special reference to obviate these defects.

The swift clippers left the ocean behind them with the fine clean wake of a surgeon's scalpel, marking the smoothness of their passage. Art, and supreme art it was, and nerve and skill, went into their sailing.
—Felix Riesenberg

THE MARKS OF THE AMERICAN CLIPPER SHIP, GENERALLY SPEAKING

Long, sharp bow, generally with considerable flare, and a hollow entrance
Raked stem
Long, lean hull
Long, clean run
Rounded bilge
Tumblehome—from slight to extreme
Vertical sternpost
Small counter
Gently sweeping sheerline, higher at the bow than the stern
Hardwood construction
Raked masts
Great press of sail

The conventions of design that establish the correct appearance of the clipper bow were developed in early times, and these conventions are as absolute as those of the classical orders in architecture.
—Howard I. Chapelle

FROM "THE BUILDING OF A SHIP"
*Built for freight, and yet for speed,
A beautiful and gallant craft;
Broad in the beam, that the stress of the blast,
Pressing down upon sail and mast,
Might not the sharp bows overwhelm;
Broad in the beam, but sloping aft
With graceful curve and slow degrees,
That she might be docile to the helm,
And that the currents of parted seas,
Closing behind, with mighty force,
Might aid and not impede her course.*
—Henry Wadsworth Longfellow

THE CLIPPER SHIP *LIGHTNING*, NORTH ATLANTIC OCEAN NEAR IRELAND, MARCH 1, 1854

Wind S., strong gales; bore away for the North Channel, carried away the foretopsail and lost jib; hove the log several times, and found the ship going through the water at the rate of 18 to 18½ knots per hour; lee rail under water, and the rigging slack; saw the Irish land at 9:30 p.m. Distance run in the twenty-four hours, 436 miles.
—from the abstract log

*The merry seamen laughed to see
Their gallant ship so lustily
Furrow the green sea foam.*
            —Sir Walter Scott

FEB/MAR

Monday
24

1836—Winslow Homer, painter of *Eight Bells* and *Gulf Stream*, as well as hundreds of other works with a marine theme, was born in Boston, Massachusetts.

Tuesday
25

1873—Arthur John Trevor Briscoe, marine artist, was born in Birkenhead, England.

Wednesday
26

1944—Sue Sophia Dauser became the first woman to achieve the rank of captain in the U.S. Navy.

Thursday
27

1813—The delivery of mail by steamboat was authorized by the U.S. Congress.

Friday
28

1944—The SS *United Victory*, the first ship of the Victory type, was launched.

Saturday
1 ST. DAVID'S DAY / UK

1854—The clipper ship *Lightning* set a record to date for the longest distance run in 24 hours—436 miles.

Sunday
2

1779—A code of articles, 50 in all, was adopted for the regulation of American naval forces.

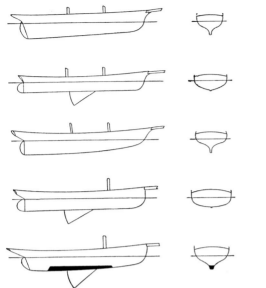
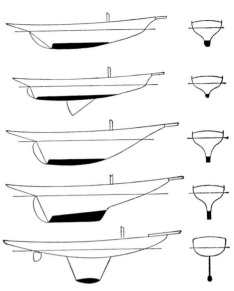

WHEN CONSIDERING THE DESIGN OF A BOAT, KEEP THESE POINTS IN MIND

All boat designs are an amalgam of compromises and should be judged in that light.

All boat designs have been influenced by those that came before.

All reviewers of boat designs are subjective, and what they have to say should be judged according to your own knowledge and experience.

All beautiful boats are not necessarily good, and all good boats are not necessarily beautiful.

CHOICES, CHOICES, CHOICES….

A vessel must be light enough to be driven easily by a moderate breeze, stiff enough to stand up to her canvas in a hard wind, shallow enough to be docked with ease and to run with speed. She must have depth enough to hold her up to windward, breadth enough to give her stability; she should be long enough to reach well, and short enough to turn well to windward; low in the water so as not to hold too much wind, with plenty of freeboard to keep the sea off her decks…. She must be broad, narrow, long, short, deep, shallow, tender, stiff…. It is not strange that designers pass sleepless nights, and that anything like finality and perfection of type is impossible to conceive.
—Lord Dunraven

Do not sacrifice the utility of the yacht for the purpose for which she is intended, to style.
—Charles G. Davis

There is no royal road to style. It cannot be obtained by mere industry; it can never be achieved through imitation, although it may be promoted by example.
—Samuel Eliot Morison

THE MOST INFLUENTIAL 20TH-CENTURY BOOKS ON AMERICAN YACHT DESIGN, TRADITIONAL STYLE

The Common Sense of Yacht Design,
  by L. Francis Herreshoff
Skene's Elements of Yacht Design,
  revised by Francis S. Kinney
Yacht Designing and Planning,
  by Howard I. Chapelle

THE LIBERTY SHIP *JOHN JAY*, NORTH ATLANTIC, MARCH 4–7, 1943

March 4. Two ships in convoy collided and returned to port. Two depth charges dropped by destroyer on forward port side of convoy. General alarm sounded. Destroyer on port side of convoy firing machine guns.

March 6. Sighted life raft on port beam. Notified destroyer.

March 7. Two 45 degree turns to port. Submarine alert. Two white rockets fired from ship on starboard side of convoy. Sounded general alarm.
—Lieutenant (j.g.) Earl G. Hardt, USN, Armed Guard

There is nothing more enticing, disenchanting, and enslaving than the life at sea.
—Joseph Conrad

MARCH

Monday
3

1823—The first bill providing appropriations for harbor improvements in the United States was passed by Congress.

Tuesday
4   SHROVE TUESDAY / UK

1918—The collier *Cyclops* sailed from Barbados, West Indies, never to be seen again. Some suggest she was swallowed up by mysterious "forces" in the so-called Bermuda Triangle.

Wednesday
5   ASH WEDNESDAY

1962—A major storm worked its way up the U.S. east coast from Florida to Maine; with high winds driving waves as high as 40 feet, coupled with seasonally high tides, there was considerable shoreline erosion, especially along the mid-Atlantic.

Thursday
6

1862—The USS *Monitor* departed New York Harbor for Hampton Roads, Virginia, and her appointment with the CSS *Virginia*, ex-USS *Merrimac*.

Friday
7

1958—The USS *Grayback*, the first submarine of the U.S. Navy built from the keel up with the capability to fire guided missiles, was commissioned.

Saturday
8

1889—Captain John Ericsson, inventor of the screw propeller and builder of the USS *Monitor*, died in New York City.

Sunday
9

The cruising of a boat here and there is very much what happens to the soul of man in a larger way.
—Hilaire Belloc

FROM *SONGS FOR ALL SEAS, ALL SHIPS*

Flaunt out O sea your separate flags of nations!
Flaunt out visible as ever the various ship-signals!
But do you reserve especially for yourself and
*   for the soul of man one flag above all the rest,*
A spiritual woven signal for all nations,
*   emblem of man elate above death,*
Token of all brave captains and all intrepid
*   sailors and mates,*
And all that went down doing their duty,
Reminiscent of them, twined from all intrepid
*   captains young or old,*
A pennant universal, subtly waving all time,
*   o'er all brave sailors,*
All seas, all ships.
                                —Walt Whitman

FLAGS AND PENNANTS OF THE INTERNATIONAL CODE

Flags are of 29 unique designs representing the letters of the alphabet and three substitutes. Letters A and B are swallowtailed; the remaining 24 letters are squared-off at the fly; the three substitutes are triangular.

Pennants are of 11 unique designs representing the numerals 0 through 9, plus the Code and Answering pennant; all are tapered, and squared-off at the fly.

SIGNALING WITH FLAGS

The sending vessel makes up the signal and hoists it close up (fully hoisted).

The receiving vessel hoists the Answering Pennant at the dip (hoisted halfway) to indicate the signal has been seen; once the receiving vessel has deciphered the message—that is, understands the signal's meaning—it brings the Answering Pennant close up.

A SHORT STORY IN FLAG SIGNAL CODE, COMPOSED FROM THE REGULATIONS OF THE EASTERN YACHT CLUB, MARBLEHEAD, MASSACHUSETTS, 1914

    FT—Wish to communicate with you
    Y—Come within hail
    BW—Where are you from?
    QS—Hampton Roads, Virginia
    BU—Where are you bound?
    NH—Bar Harbor, Maine
    GC—Will you lunch with me?
    C—Yes
    GI—And bring your guests
    FW—Thank you
    GF, JA—Will meet you at the Club at noon
    GJ—Send a boat for me
    GW—At once

THE U.S. FRIGATE *CONSTELLATION*, NEAR GUADELOUPE, MARCH 12, 1799

Moderate Breezes, and fair Weather with smooth Water. At 6 AM saw a Ship of War in our Wake, standing after us; tacked and stood towards her, and then made the British private Signal for the Day, which she answered, and immediately after she thru out the British Frigate *Lapwing*'s private Signal as fixt between us, when I in Return hoisted my private Signal, which being understood by her, and our Ensigns respectively having been displayed, each stood on his own Course: ...All hands employed repairing Rigging, and doing various other Jobs, that are necessary to keep in good Order the Apparatus, Tackle, and all the Appurtenances of every Department.
                        —Captain Thomas Truxton

The shore, to me, was merely a place where one occasionally had to go to fill up with stores.
—Peter Gerard

MARCH

Monday 10
COMMONWEALTH DAY / UK

If sail you must, take my advice: never trust all you possess on board of a ship. —Hesiod

Tuesday 11

1924—The six-masted schooner *Wyoming*, the largest wooden schooner ever built—329 feet length, 50 feet beam, 30 feet draft—sank east of the Pollock Rip Lightship, Cape Cod; there were no survivors.

Wednesday 12

1822—Pietro Riva, founder of the Riva boatyard, builder of some of the finest wooden speedboats and runabouts in the world, was born in Laglio, Italy.

Thursday 13

1841—The steamer *President*, en route from New York to Liverpool with 136 people on board, was struck by a storm on this date and never heard from again.

Friday 14

1868—The Millwall Docks on the River Thames, London, were officially opened.

Saturday 15

1983—The last propeller-driven U.S. Coast Guard aircraft in search and rescue service, an HC-131A Samaritan, was retired.

Sunday 16

1887—The New Zealand Amateur Rowing Association, a union of nine clubs, was founded.

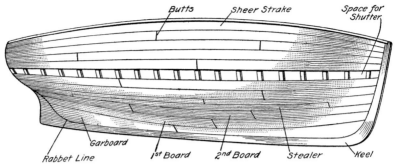

*T*he desire to build a boat is one of those that cannot be resisted. It begins as a little cloud on a serene horizon. It ends by covering the whole sky, so that you can think of nothing else. You must build to regain your freedom.
—Arthur Ransome

THE WEIGHT OF WOODS FOR BOAT WORK, IN POUNDS PER CUBIC FOOT, 12 PERCENT MOISTURE CONTENT

    Locust, 48
    White oak, 47
    Red oak, 44
    Ash, 41
    Yellow pine, 41
    Walnut, 38
    Hackmatack, 36
    Cherry, 35
    Elm, 35
    Cypress, 32
    Alaska cedar, 31
    Port Orford cedar, 29
    Redwood, 28
    Sitka spruce, 28
    Eastern white spruce, 28
    Douglas-fir, 27
    Eastern white pine, 25
    Southern white cedar, 23
    Western cedar, 23
    Northern white cedar, 22

*B*etter timber for a ship than pasture white oak never grew.
—Joshua Slocum

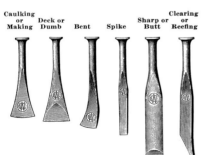

THE BASICS OF CAULKING A CARVEL-PLANKED HULL

Seams should be V-shaped in cross-section, tightly closed at the back of the V and open at the front approximately 1/8 inch for each inch of plank thickness.

For ease in working, right-handed caulkers work from left to right; left-handers, from right to left.

First lightly tuck short loops of cotton in the seam—wide seams: more loops closer together; narrow seams: fewer loops wider apart—then go back and harden them down with sharp blows of the mallet. The cotton should be driven below the edges of the seam to make room for seam compound.

Paint the seams with an oil-based paint.

After the paint has dried, fill the seams with flexible seam compound or putty.

Note: The cotton makes the seams waterproof; the compound is there to hold the cotton in place and to make the hull smooth.

*T*here is but a plank between a sailor and eternity.
—Thomas Gibbons

THE WHALESHIP *ATHOL*, SANDWICH ISLANDS (HAWAII), MARCH 20, 1847

The pilot took us into a snug little harbour protected from the sea by coral reefs, and we came to anchor in five fathoms of water, off the town of Honolulu, a cable's length from the shore. The captain asked the pilot where he could find comfortable lodgings for himself and family, and was rather astonished to learn that there was neither hotel nor boarding house in the town.... There was but one wharf, and that did not extend out to deep water. Only a vessel of very light draft could lie to it, and it served chiefly as a landing place for boats.
—Benjamin Doane

Father, father, build me a boat
Out on the ocean I will float.
          —from an old sea song

MARCH

Monday
17 ST. PATRICK'S DAY

1902—All but one of the crew of the Monomoy (Massachusetts) Life-Saving Station were lost while attempting to rescue the crew of a wrecked coal barge.

Tuesday
18

1969—Bernard Moitessier, in first place in the first round-the-world race for singlehanded sailors, dropped out after crossing his outbound track and continued on to the Pacific islands.

Wednesday
19

1917—The U.S. Navy authorized the enlistment of women in the Naval Reserve.

Thursday
20

1922—Restoration began on HMS *Victory*, Admiral Lord Nelson's flagship at the battle of Trafalgar in 1805; she is now permanently drydocked in Portsmouth, England.

Friday
21 VERNAL EQUINOX

1905—The four-masted bark *Archibald Russell*, the last square-rigger of hundreds built on the River Clyde in Scotland, got underway on her maiden voyage.

Saturday
22

1915—Naval Aviator replaced Navy Air Pilot as the designation for fliers in the U.S. Navy.

Sunday
23

1929—*Miss America VII*, driven by Gar Wood, set a world propeller-driven water speed record to date of 93.123 mph, at Miami Beach, Florida.

*There was an old man in a boat,
Who said, 'I'm afloat, I'm afloat!'
When they said, 'No you ain't!'
He was ready to faint,
That unhappy old man in a boat.*
—Edward Lear

Just because small craft are small does not make them any less a joy. —John Gardner

HERE'S WHAT YOU SHOULD ALWAYS HAVE ABOARD A SMALL, OPEN DAYSAILER BEYOND THE MINIMUM LEGAL REQUIREMENTS

Oars	Paddle	Compass
Oarlocks	Boathook	Flashlight
Container of fresh water		

THE SAILING CANOE *YAKABOO*, LESSER ANTILLES, MARCH 30, 1911

I had scarcely got her under way and was still under the lee of the land when the first sea came, like the hoary hand of Neptune himself and we turned to meet it. Aft I slid, she lifted her bow—just enough—and the sea broke under us—and we dropped down its steep back, with lighter hearts. In with the mainsheet and we were off again, the canoe tearing along like a scared cotton-tail—a little white bunch under her stern. There was something worth while in this and I kept my eyes to weather for the next sea. Again we met it and came through triumphant. Perhaps I had not erred after all.
—Frederic Fenger

WHEN SAILING A SMALL BOAT IN A SEAWAY

Position all weight, including crew and passengers, as near the center of the boat, and as low down, as possible.

Reduce sail area to lower the angle of heel.

Do not allow anyone to move about, or stand on the deck, or sit on the gunwale.

RUNNING BEFORE A HEAVY SEA IN A SMALL SAILING BOAT

Reduce sail.

Take up on the topping lift to keep the boom from striking the waves.

Haul up the centerboard, or take it at least halfway up.

If the boat is running too fast, throw a drag on a long line overboard; a drogue if you have one, or an oar, a thwart, a floorboard, or even a seat cushion.

Concentrate on steering to prevent a broach.

SAILING A SMALL BOAT IN A STRONG BEAM SEA

Don't do it if at all possible.

Reduce sail to prevent excessive heeling.

To reduce pressure in a puff, do not luff up; rather, ease the sheet and bear off.

In heavy going, zigzag, or quarter, the seas.

A good boat is no more seaworthy than her crew—in other words, skill of handling is part of seaworthiness in small craft.
—Howard I. Chapelle

MARCH

Monday
24

1989—The supertanker *Exxon Valdez* grounded on a reef in Prince William Sound, Alaska, spilling 10.1 million gallons of crude oil, the worst such accident in U.S. history.

Tuesday
25

1947—The SS *St. Lawrence Victory* struck a mine left over from World War II and sank, thus becoming the last-known U.S. ship to be lost as the result of that war.

Wednesday
26

1773—Nathaniel Bowditch, mariner, mathematician, astronomer, author of the *American Practical Navigator*, was born in Salem, Massachusetts.

Thursday
27

1880—The U.S. sloop-of-war *Constellation* sailed from New York Harbor with food to help relieve the Irish potato famine.

Friday
28

1819—The auxiliary steamer *Savannah*, which would become the first steam-powered vessel to cross the Atlantic, got underway on her maiden voyage from Connecticut to Georgia.

Saturday
29

1957—Ralph E. Winslow, yacht designer best known for his powerboats and auxiliary sailboats, died in Quincy, Massachusetts.

Sunday
30
MOTHERING SUNDAY / UK
BRITISH SUMMER TIME BEGINS / UK

THE SAILING SHIP *CANTON*, ATLANTIC OCEAN EAST OF VIRGINIA, APRIL 6, 1800

At nine saw a sail to wind'd. At 10 spoke her—ye sloop *Hannah* of and for Boston 7 days from ye Island of Cuba—informs that no actual declaration of war has taken place between us and France—that our beloved Washington is no more & that the *Constitution* frigate, Capt. Talbot has sunk a French frigate, and was towed disabled into Jamaica.
—Commander Richard Dale

THE GAM, DEFINED BY HERMAN MELVILLE

What does the whaler do when she meets another whaler in any sort of decent weather? She has a Gam, a thing so utterly unknown to all other ships that they never heard of the name even....

With that view, let me learnedly define it. Gam. Noun—A social meeting of two (or more) Whale-ships, generally on a cruising-ground; when, after exchanging hails, they exchange visits by boats' crews: the two captains remaining, for the time, on board of one ship, and the two chief mates on the other.

"To gam"...is a substitute for the verbs "to visit," "to gossip." It expresses the garrulity of the sea, and is a pleasant break in the monotony of the life.
—Jack London

THE GAM, ALAS, IS OVER

The time was when ships passing one another at sea backed their topsails and had a "gam," and on parting fired guns; but those good old days have gone. People have hardly time nowadays to speak even on the broad ocean, where news is news, and as for a salute of guns, they cannot afford the powder. There are no poetry-enshrined freighters on the sea now; it is a prosy life when we have no time to bid one another good morning.
—Joshua Slocum

SHIPS THAT PASS IN THE NIGHT
by Henry Wadsworth Longfellow

Ships that pass in the night, and speak each other in passing,
Only a signal shown and a distant voice in the darkness;
So on the ocean of life we pass and speak one another,
Only a look and a voice, then dirtiness again and a silence.

WHEN TWO SAILING VESSELS ARE APPROACHING ONE ANOTHER, SO AS TO INVOLVE RISK OF COLLISION, ONE OF THEM SHALL KEEP OUT OF THE WAY OF THE OTHER AS FOLLOWS:

- when each has the wind on a different side, the vessel which has the wind on the port side shall keep out of the way of the other;
- when both have the wind on the same side, the vessel which is to windward shall keep out of the way of the vessel which is to leeward;
- if a vessel with the wind on the port side sees a vessel to windward and cannot determine with certainty whether the other vessel has the wind on the port or on the starboard side, she shall keep out of the way of the other.

—International Regulations for Prevention of Collisions at Sea

There is really something strangely cheering to the spirits in the meeting of a ship at sea.
—Benjamin Franklin

MAR/APRIL

Monday
31

1952—Regular ferry service across the Delaware River from Philadelphia to Camden, New Jersey, which had been in continuous operation for 250 years, was discontinued.

Tuesday
1
APRIL FOOLS' DAY

1967—The U.S. Coast Guard became part of the newly established Department of Transportation after nearly 177 years in the Treasury Department.

Wednesday
2

1827—Construction began on the first naval hospital in the United States, in Portsmouth, Virginia.

Thursday
3

1980—Two supertankers, the *Albahaa* and the *Mycene*, exploded and burned within hours of each other on opposite coasts of Africa.

Friday
4

1818—The first steamboat on the Great Lakes, the *Walk-in-the-Water*, was launched in Buffalo, New York.

Saturday
5

1621—The Pilgrim ship *Mayflower* departed the Plymouth colony, Massachusetts, on her return voyage to England.

Sunday
6
DAYLIGHT SAVINGS BEGINS / US & CANADA

FASTEST SAILING-SHIP PASSAGES, NEW YORK TO SAN FRANCISCO

89 days, 4 hours—clipper *Andrew Jackson*, December 1859 to March 1860

89 days, 8 hours—clipper *Flying Cloud*, January to April 1854

FASTEST SAILING-SHIP PASSAGES, SAN FRANCISCO TO NEW YORK

76 days, 7 hours—clipper *Comet*, December 1853 to March 1854

79 days—clipper *Bald Eagle*, March to May 1854

SPEED CONVERSIONS

To convert	Into	Multiply by
kilometers/hour	knots	0.5396
knots	statute miles/hour	1.151

THE CLIPPER
by Thomas Fleming Day

Her sails are strong and yellow as the sand,
Her spars are tall and supple as the pine,
And, like the bounty of a generous mine,
Sun-touched, her brasses flash on every hand.
Her sheer takes beauty from a golden band,
Which, sweeping aft, is taught to twist and twine
Into a scroll, and badge of quaint design
Hang on her quarters. Insolent and grand
She drives. Her stem rings loudly as it throws
The hissing sapphire into foamy waves,
While on her weather bends the copper glows
In burnished splendor. Rolling down she laves
Her high black sides until the scupper flows,
Then pushing out her shapely bow she braves
The next tall sea, and, leaping, onward goes.

THE CLIPPER SHIP *STAG HOUND*, PACIFIC OCEAN, NEAR VALPARAISO, APRIL 7, 1851

We are now sixty-days out, and I feel very confident that you will hear of us at San Francisco in a hundred days from New York. If our ship's spars had only kept in their places, we should doubtless have made the passage in ninety days. The *Stag Hound* has proved herself to be an excellent seaboat; and as to her sailing, I do not believe there is a ship afloat that she could not beat with ease. We overtake and pass vessels, one after another, almost as if they were lying at anchor.

—a passenger

If one does not know to which port one is sailing, no wind is favorable.
—Seneca

APRIL

Monday
7

1883—The steam yacht *Atalanta*, owned by financier Jay Gould, considered by many to have been the finest yacht built to date in the United States, was launched in Philadelphia.

Tuesday
8

1861—The extreme clipper ship *Witchcraft* drove ashore at Chickamaconic, North Carolina; 15 lives were lost.

Wednesday
9

1877—A northeaster with high winds, waves, and tides caused significant erosion along the mid-Atlantic coast; Oregon Inlet, North Carolina, was widened by three-quarters of a mile.

Thursday
10

1904—The first issue of *Motor Boat*, the first magazine devoted exclusively to the new sport of motorboating, was published.

Friday
11

1974—*Great Britain II*, skippered by Chay Blyth, was first to finish in the first Whitbread Round the World Race; winner on corrected time was *Sayula II*.

Saturday
12

1934—A wind gust of 231 mph was recorded on Mount Washington, New Hampshire, a world record.

Sunday
13 PALM SUNDAY

Speed on the ship!
—John Greenleaf Whittier

SEAGOING WORDS TAKEN FROM HUMAN ANATOMY

Arm—part of an anchor
Belly—the part of a sail that bulges out from the pressure of the wind
Bottom—underside of the hull
Breast—docking line leading at an angle of 90 degrees from the side of a vessel
Brow—gangplank
Bum—two-masted lateen-rigged craft of the Arabian region; aka boom
Butt—end-to-end planking joint
Buttock—line representing a vertical section of a hull parallel to the centerline
Cheek—side piece of a block
Chest—box containing cargo, usually tea
Chin—lower portion of a vessel's stem
Elbow—curve in a river or channel
Eye—loop at the end of a line
Foot—lower edge of a sail
Hand—member of the crew
Head—forward part of a vessel; also the toilet
Heel—lowest part of the mast
Knee—angle used to connect timbers or beams
Knuckle—sharp angle or bend in a hull
Lip—coaming
Mouth—opening to a bay, harbor, river, etc.
Neck—part of an oar where the loom or shaft meets the blade
Nose—stem of a vessel
Palm—part of an anchor; also a sailmaker's tool
Rib—frame
Shin—to climb a mast, rope, or spar
Shoulder—projection on a block or mast
Throat—the forward or inner end of a gaff; the corner of a gaff sail between the head and the luff
Tongue—block of wood between the jaws of a gaff
Waist—central part of a vessel

THE HAND AT SEA

Hand—a unit of measure: 4 inches
Hand—a member of the crew
Lend a hand—help me (a request)
Bear a hand—help me (an order)
All hands!—all members of the crew assemble

A LANDING PARTY FROM HMS *BEAGLE*, CAPE HORN, APRIL 18–19, 1830

I afterward went in a boat to Horn Island, to ascertain the nature of the landing, and whether it was practicable to carry any instruments to the summit of the Cape. Many places were found where a boat might land; more than one spot where she could be hauled ashore; so that taking instruments to the summit did not seem likely to be a very difficult task. As the weather continued favourable I returned on board that night and the next morning arranged for a visit to Cape Horn.... After taking observations at noon for latitude, we set out, carrying five days' provisions, a good chronometer, and other instruments. We landed before dark, hauled our boat up in safety on the northeast side, and established ourselves for the night on Horn Island.

—Captain Robert Fitzroy, R.N.

It is easier for us to go down to the sea in a small ship than to remain on dry land.
—Jack London

APRIL

Monday
14

1944—The British ammunition ship *Fort Stikene* blew up in the port of Bombay, India, killing almost 1,000 people, burning the entire dock area, sinking 12 ships, and seriously damaging 12 more.

Tuesday
15

1851—Donald McKay's clipper ship *Flying Cloud*, perhaps the most famous of the type, was launched in East Boston, Massachusetts.

Wednesday
16

1934—The J-class yacht *Endeavour*, owned by T.O.M. Sopwith, unsuccessful challenger for the *America*'s Cup, was launched in Gosport, England.

Thursday
17 PASSOVER

1893—The clipper ship *Nightingale*, named after the singer Jenny Lind, "The Swedish Nightingale," was abandoned in the North Atlantic Ocean and was lost.

Friday
18 GOOD FRIDAY

1775—Paul Revere crossed by rowboat from Boston to Charlestown, Massachusetts, on the first leg of his famous ride to Lexington.

Saturday
19

1861—President Abraham Lincoln proclaimed that all Confederate privateers would be treated by Union authorities as pirates.

Sunday
20 EASTER SUNDAY

1861—The Norfolk Navy Yard, Virginia, was abandoned by Union forces and burned.

By and by I ran away. I said I never would come home again till I was a pilot and could come in glory.
—Mark Twain

PILOT
A person with local knowledge who is licensed to guide vessels into and out of a particular harbor or channel, during which time he or she is in absolute command of the vessel. In French, *pilote*; in German, *lotse*. Also, a book of piloting instructions, aka sailing directions, such as the U.S. Coast Pilot. The word *pilot* is thought to have derived from the Dutch *peillood*, meaning sounding lead, once the principal tool of pilotage.

PILOTAGE
The art of coastal navigation.

*To heave the lead the seaman spring,
And to the pilot cheerly sung,
"By the deep—nine!"*
—Charles Dibdin

Taking on a pilot

A SHIP FROM MALDONADA FOR LUGGNAGG, APRIL 21, 1708
We sailed into the river of Clumegnig, which is a seaport town, at the south-east point of Luggnagg. We cast anchor within a league of the town, and made a signal for a pilot. Two of them came on board in less than half an hour, by whom we were guided between certain shoals and rocks, which are very dangerous in the passage, to a large basin, where a fleet may ride in safety within a cable's length of the town-wall.

Some of our sailors, whether out of treachery or inadvertence, had informed the pilots "that I was a stranger, and great traveller"; whereof these gave notice to a custom-house officer, by whom I was examined very strictly upon my landing. This officer spoke to me in the language of Balnibarbi, which, by the force of much commerce, is generally understood in that town, especially by seamen and those employed in the customs.
—Gulliver

PILOT, OR PEA, COAT
Woolen coat originally favored by North Sea pilots and eventually adopted by sailors and yachtsmen for its warmth and weather resistance. The current term, *pea coat*, is derived from the cloth used—pilot-, or p-cloth.

PILOT-CLOTH
A thick, blue, woolen twill cloth, napped on one side.

PILOT DIRECTIONS FOR ENTERING THE RIO GRANDE, BRAZIL, 1845
When you make the tower, endeavor to get it to bear N., five or six miles distant; then steer directly for it, but be particular to observe if a red flag be hoisted on the tower: if so, it signifies that you must approach and continue to advance (as long as the flag is up) direct for the tower, until you see a boat, which will be at anchor on the bar, in which a pilot will be situated.... Steer for the boat, guiding yourself by a staff with a flag, which is inclined by the man in the boat, as follows:—If the staff be held upright, you are steering correctly; if the staff be inclined to port or starboard, you must luff or keep off accordingly.

But soon I heard the dash of oars,
I heard the Pilot's cheer....
—Samuel Taylor Coleridge

APRIL

Monday
21 EASTER MONDAY / UK & CANADA

1861—The clipper ship *Nightingale*, then engaged in the slave trade, was captured by the USS *Saratoga* off Kabinda (now a province of Angola), Africa.

Tuesday
22

1969—Robin Knox-Johnston, the first singlehander to circumnavigate the globe nonstop, returned to Falmouth, England, aboard the yacht *Suhaili*.

Wednesday
23 ST. GEORGE'S DAY / UK

1934—More than 100 ships of the U.S. Navy passed through the Panama Canal, a record to date.

Thursday
24

1961—The 64-gun ship *Vasa*, sunk in 1628, was raised from the bottom of Stockholm Harbor, Sweden. After years of restoration and conservation, she is now a historical exhibit.

Friday
25

1808—Foreign vessels were forbidden by the government of the United States to engage in the American coasting trade.

Saturday
26

1991—A reproduction (the second) of the colonial ship *Susan Constant* was commissioned at the Jamestown Settlement, near Williamsburg, Virginia.

Sunday
27

1521—Ferdinand Magellan was murdered by natives at Mactan Island, Philippines.

*T*here's a tempest in
 yon horned moon,
And lightning in yon
 cloud,
And hard the music,
 mariners,
The wind is piping
 loud;
The wind is piping
 loud, my boys!
The lightning flashes
 free,
While the hollow oak
 our palace is,
Our heritage the sea.
  —from "A Wet Sheet and a Flowing Sea,"
    Allan Cunningham

TO DETERMINE HOW FAR AWAY A FLASH OF LIGHTNING IS FROM YOU

Count the seconds between the sight of the flash and the sound of the thunder.

Divide by five.

The result is distance in miles.

If the flash and sound are instantaneous, the lightning discharge is close by.

If the lightning discharge is 15 miles or more from the observer, no thunder will be heard.

THE COLIN ARCHER CUTTER *TEDDY*, BAY OF PANAMA, APRIL 28, 1929

The night, moonless and densely clouded, had settled around us with pitchy darkness. One could not see a hand held before the eyes. Rain came down in torrents. Repeatedly it drowned the riding light, until I abandoned the attempt of relighting it. Only the binnacle lamp was burning, throwing its faint rays on the cockpit combing, on a hand that was groping for a sheet rope or on a shining black oilskin coat.

And then the tempest broke loose. Crackling lightning bore down from out of greenish-brown poisonous-looking clouds, that crowded low above the phosphorescent masthead. In ever quicker succession it swished down into the sea to right and left, some of the flashes in the immediate vicinity of the quivering boat, while the incessant roar of thunder, deafening the ear, shattering the nerves, sounded like hell let loose, like the infernal gunfire of a million gigantic demons at war.
  —Erling Tambs

HOW LONG WILL A THUNDERSTORM LAST?

If the wind comes before the rain, the dirty weather will be over quickly.

If the rain precedes the wind, the thunderstorm is likely just the beginning of a longer spell of dirty weather.

WHEN A THUNDERSTORM ARISES

Get off the water if at all possible. If not, and if in a sailboat, douse the sails—headsails first—and lash them securely.

Anchor if possible, but not on a lee shore; if not possible, prepare to run under bare poles or, at most, a small jib.

If in an open boat, don't stand up and become a lightning rod; stay low, and keep your hands and feet out of the water.

If in a boat with a cabin, get below and stay in the middle of the largest space.

Disconnect electronic equipment, and don't touch it during the storm.

Lower or remove antennas.

There is no dallying nor excuses with stormes, gusts, overgrowne Seas, and lee-shores.
—Captain John Smith

APRIL/MAY

Monday
28

1884—Joseph Conrad signed as second mate aboard the square-rigger *Narcissus* on a voyage from Bombay, India, to London; the vessel was to figure in Conrad's immortal work *The Nigger of the* Narcissus.

Tuesday
29

1973—The Mississippi River crested at 43.4 feet, the highest to date; the previous high was 42 feet, set in 1785.

Wednesday
30

1942—The USS *Peto*, the first submarine to be built on the Great Lakes, was launched.

Thursday
1

1998—The amphibious tour boat *Miss Majestic* sank in Lake Hamilton, Hot Springs, Arkansas, drowning 13 people.

Friday
2

1835—The Hudson's Bay Company's *Beaver*, the first steamship on the West Coast of North America, was launched at Blackwall, River Thames, London, England.

Saturday
3

1891—Steamer deck chairs, leased to steamship companies, were introduced by Heinrich Conried of the Ocean Company.

Sunday
4

1861—The first gun for the fledgling Navy of the Confederate States of America was cast at the Phoenix Iron Works, Gretna, Louisiana.

EXPRESSIVE SLANG, ROYAL NAVY, MID-TWENTIETH CENTURY

Anchor the arse—sit down
Better than a slap in the belly with a wet fish—things could be worse
Churchill's chicken—corned beef
Deep sea beef—haddock
Ecclesiastical brick—holystone, aka prayer book, used for scrubbing the deck
Floating Fifth Avenue—passenger liner
Grog blossoms—red cheeks from too much rum
Hang out the wash—set sail
In the house—serving as mess cook
Jump off the dock—get married
King's parade—the quarterdeck
Lamp-post navigation—proceed from buoy to buoy in poor visibility
Mechanized dandruff—head lice
Nose-ender—wind from dead ahead
Odds and sods—the rank and file of the Royal Navy
Piss-pot jerker—cabin steward on a passenger liner
Quack—ship's surgeon
Rock chasing—navigation exercises
She has lines like a butter-box—that vessel is ugly
Tonsil varnish—low-grade tea
Underground fruit—potatoes, carrots, radishes, etc.
Vicarage—chaplain's cabin aboard ship
Work double tides—perform extra duty
X-chaser—someone who is mathematically inclined
Yachtsman's gale—strong breeze that the navyman would regard with indifference
Zeppelins in a fog—sausages and mashed potatoes

A BIBLIOGRAPHY OF SAILORS' SLANG

Sailors' Language, by W. Clark Russell, 1883
Soldier and Sailor Words and Phrases, by Edward Fraser and John Gibbons, 1925
Sea Slang, by Frank C. Bowen, 1929
Royal Navalese, by Commander John Irving, 1946
Sea Slang of the Twentieth Century, by Wilfred Granville, 1949
The Sailor's Word Book, by Admiral W.H. Smyth, 1967

THE 26-FOOT SCHOONER CIMBA, NEAR TAHITI, MAY 6, 1935

Morning, with no land in sight, with the sea silent under grey cloud and given over to what old-time crews would have called a "clock" calm or a Paddy's hurricane—an "up-and-down wind" that had disappeared "walking Spanish." Although clouds were lighted by "devil's smiles" of sunlight piercing their wetness, the weather became dense, visibility was lost, a confused sea started to throw up, and before long a rainy "nose-ender" was wailing over the bows. Strange South Seas weather! The rigging tautened, the dead-work buried under to the wash-boards, and with sails flat, bows a-pitch and flushing, the *Cimba* dived into a hollow, curling sea.

—Richard Maury

*The slang of the seafarer must ever be
the despair of a glossographer.*
—Wilfred Granville

MAY

Monday
5   BANK HOLIDAY / UK

1945—The SS *Black Point* was lost five miles off the coast of Rhode Island, the last ship to be sunk by a German U-boat.

Tuesday
6

1936—The U.S. Congress authorized the construction, in Carderock, Maryland, of the David Taylor Model Basin for the tank-testing of hull shapes.

Wednesday
7

1934—William Gardner, designer of some of the finest yachts of his time, including the three-masted schooner *Atlantic*, which held the transatlantic speed record under sail, died in Bay Head, New Jersey.

Thursday
8

1911—On a day considered the birthday of naval aviation, the U.S. Navy placed an order for its first airplane, a Curtiss A-1.

Friday
9

1837—The steamboat *Ben Sherrod*, while engaged in a race with the steamboat *Prairie*, caught fire and burned 30 miles below Natchez, Mississippi; 175 lives were lost.

Saturday
10

1859—William Gardner, yacht designer, was born in Oswego, New York.

Sunday
11   MOTHER'S DAY / US & CANADA

A RIVER IN THE OCEAN, DESCRIBED BY LIEUTENANT MATTHEW FONTAINE MAURY, USN

There is a river in the ocean. In the severest droughts it never fails, and in the mightiest floods it never overflows—It is the Gulf Stream.

HOW TO BENEFIT FROM THE GULF STREAM, ACCORDING TO BENJAMIN FRANKLIN

A vessel from Europe to North America may shorten her passage by avoiding to stem the stream…; and a vessel from America to Europe may do the same by the same means of keeping in it. It may often have happened accidentally, that voyages have been shortened by these circumstances. It is now well to have the command of them.

CROSSING THE STREAM

Crossing the Gulf Stream, especially in a small boat, should never be taken lightly. Off the east coast of the United States, the Stream—a river without banks—moves generally north and east, and when the wind blows against it, can throw up steep, nasty, overwhelming waves. To avoid problems:
- Never begin a crossing in winds with the word "north" in them (north, northeast, northwest), or when such winds are forecast.
- Never set a course against the direction of the Stream's current.
- Watch assiduously for your weather window of opportunity; when it comes, take it.

OUT OF THE STREAM

At 2 p.m., temperature of the water had fallen seven degrees in half an hour—from 72 degrees down to 65 degrees. Already the day is turning cold…. At 2:30, temperature of water two degrees lower—viz., 63 degrees. At 3, it was 61 degrees. It fell eleven degrees in an hour and a half. Then we passed out, and the weather turned bitter cold.

—Mark Twain

THE PACKET SHIP *GARRICK*, ATLANTIC OCEAN, CROSSING THE GULF STREAM, MAY 13, 1854

Noon, lat. 40 degrees 5 minutes N., long. 63 degrees 21 minutes W. Pleasant though sultry. About 4 p.m. the water from a deep green changed to a greenish blue. A moderate swell from S.S.E. Rock and Gulf weed, wilted grass and straws. Passed during the forenoon a nautilus under swelling sail and with pliant oars, also a very singular looking mollusk, red as a lobster with 5 or 6 blunt projections and as large as a middle sized turtle. When in the stream, the agitation of the current was quick and fine, water 71 degrees of a deep ocean blue. When at 7 bells we emerged, water 68 degrees, the colour became a bluish green.

—Captain R.W. Foster

All day long, day after day,
We follow the sacred body of the river.
　　　　　　　—Elizabeth Coatsworth

MAY

Monday
12

1975—The U.S. merchant ship *Mayaguez*, accused of being a spy ship, was seized by Cambodia.

Tuesday
13

1870—The hulk of HMS *Beagle*, which had carried Charles Darwin on his voyage of scientific discovery, and most recently had been a watch vessel on the coast of Essex, England, was sold for scrap.

Wednesday
14

1986—The *Pride of Baltimore*, a reproduction of a Baltimore clipper, was knocked down by a freak squall and sank with the loss of four lives in the Atlantic Ocean north of Puerto Rico.

Thursday
15

1934—The passenger liner *Olympic*, traveling at high speed in heavy fog, ran down and sank the Nantucket Lightship; seven of the lightship crew were lost.

Friday ○
16

1806—Great Britain, in its struggle with France, declared a blockade of the European coast from Brest to the River Elbe.

Saturday
17   ARMED FORCES DAY

Sunday
18

1878—A French company secured from Colombia the right to build a ship canal across the Isthmus of Panama.

Old Slush, the sea cook

NICKNAMES FOR THE SEA COOK

Slushy	Grub-spoiler
Slush	Kitchen physic
Old Slush	Doctor

THE WHALESHIP *ENTERPRISE*, AT SEA, MAY 25, 1856

    For dinner we had a pie of some sea birds (loons they are called) and they tasted excellent. Perhaps this was owing to our appetites being somewhat sated with beef and pork on board which was all brought from Scotland. A good deal of it is fresh beef however (for hanging it up in legs about the rigging keeps it from spoiling), but for all this as a matter of course it is not half as good as when newly killed. The rest is salted and is nearly as good as the other. But the beef I can easily make myself like, but the bad water tried me most: I have to drink it with lemon juice it tastes so very bad.   —Alexander Trotter

A NAUTICAL BALLAD
by Charles Edward Carryl

*A capital ship for an ocean trip
   Was The Walloping Window-blind—
No gale that blew dismayed her crew
   Or troubled the captain's mind.
The man at the wheel was taught to feel
   Contempt for the wildest blow,
And it often appeared, when the weather had cleared,
   That he'd been in his bunk below.*

*The boatswain's mate was very sedate,
   Yet fond of amusement, too;
And he played hop-scotch with the starboard watch,
   While the captain tickled the crew.
And the gunner we had was apparently mad,
   For he sat on the after-rail,
And fired salutes with the captain's boots,
   In the teeth of the booming gale.*

*The captain sat in a commodore's hat
   And dined, in a royal way,
On toasted pigs and pickles and figs
   And gummery bread, each day.
But the cook was Dutch, and behaved as such;
   For the food that he gave the crew
Was a number of tons of hot-cross buns,
   Chopped up with sugar and glue.*

*And we all felt ill as mariners will,
   On a diet that's cheap and rude;
And we shivered and shook as we dipped the cook
   In a tub of his gluesome food.
Then nautical pride we laid aside,
   And we cast the vessel ashore
On the Gulliby Isles, where the Poohpooh smiles,
   And the Anagazanders roar.*

*Composed of sand was that favored land,
   And trimmed with cinnamon straws;
And pink and blue was the pleasing hue
   Of the Tickletoeteaser's claws.
And we sat on the edge of a sandy ledge
   And shot at the whistling bee;
And the Binnacle-bats wore water-proof hats
   As they danced in the sounding sea.*

*On rubagub bark, from dawn to dark,
   We fed, till we all had grown
Uncommonly shrunk,—when a Chinese junk
   Came by from the torriby zone.
She was stubby and square, but we didn't much care,
   And we cheerily put to sea;
And we left the crew of the junk to chew
   The bark of the rubagub tree.*

Sailing people who live in houses often envy those who live in boats.
— Anthony Bailey

MAY

Monday
19
VICTORIA DAY / CANADA

A yachtsman sails on his stomach.
— Dennis Puleston

Tuesday
20

1844—The U.S. frigate *Constitution* sailed from New York City on a round-the-world cruise.

Wednesday
21

1894—The Manchester Ship Canal, connecting the inland city of Manchester, England, with the open sea via the River Mersey, was dedicated by Queen Victoria.

Thursday
22

1865—U.S. President Andrew Johnson announced the end of the naval blockade of all southern ports.

Friday
23

1986—Don Allum of Great Britain arrived in Nevis, West Indies, at the end of a solo row across the Atlantic Ocean from Pasito Blanco, Canary Islands.

Saturday
24

1917—The first U.S. transatlantic convoy of World War I departed Hampton Roads, Virginia.

Sunday
25

1851—The clipper ship *Challenge*, the largest wooden sailing merchant vessel to date and the first with three decks, was launched in New York.

FLATIRON SKIFF

Also known as a flattie skiff or just plain skiff, the flatiron skiff is so named because it resembles an old-fashioned household flatiron. Virtually a generic American boat type, the typical flatiron is defined by a flat bottom with moderate rocker, straight stem—either plumb or raked to various degrees—moderate sheer, varying amounts of flare, and a flat, raked transom. The bottom is cross-planked, and the sides can be of a single wide plank; two or more planks set edge to edge; or two or more planks lapped. "The boats are often, and rightly, said to be easy to build but hard to design," according to Howard Chapelle.

MACKINAW BOAT

A double-ended fishing boat once common along the shores of the Great Lakes, particularly Lake Huron. An open boat, it had a straight stem, raked sternpost, straight keel, strong sheer, high bow, flattish floors, centerboard, and hogged bowsprit. The Mackinaw boat ranged in size from 25 to 35 feet in length and carried its beam forward, with a relatively fine run aft. It was gaff-rigged as either a ketch or a schooner and had an outboard rudder. Construction was either lapstrake or carvel. The type was noted for its speed and ability to handle the rough seas of the Great Lakes.

PISCATAQUA WHERRY

A dory type, the Piscataqua River wherry resembles a cross between a traditional Bank dory and the more refined knuckle-frame Swampscott dory. It has little resemblance to the English "gentleman's" wherry and none at all to the U.S. Navy's wherry. Averaging 16 feet long and with a moderate freeboard in comparison to a Bank dory, this type was once common for water transportation and inshore fishing in the tidal waters of the Piscataqua River, on the border between Maine and New Hampshire. The boats had moderate sheer, a sharply raked tombstone transom, a curved stem, and a slightly rockered bottom; at the waterline, they were virtually double-ended. They had a narrow, fore-and-aft-planked bottom, lapstrake side planking, galvanized fastenings, and as many as three rowing stations in the larger models. Perhaps the handsomest of the dory types, the Piscataqua River wherries were fast and seaworthy.

ON THE BEACH, DUNKIRK, MAY 31, 1940

Ammunition was going up like fireworks. I waded out to my armpits and scrambled aboard a boat. Two others jumped out of the boat and completely swamped her. We spent about two hours trying to re-float her, but the seas were too strong. I decided to look for a change of clothes and searched the beach, where I soon picked up some short pants and socks. On returning, I found my party gone. I picked up some biscuits on the beach and presently, when I boarded the destroyer, I had an enormous feast of bread, bully-beef and tea.

—a soldier

Germany's defeat and Europe's liberation began at Dunkirk.
—Chester Wilmot

MAY/JUNE

Monday
26
MEMORIAL DAY
SPRING BANK HOLIDAY / UK

1940—The evacuation by sea of the British Expeditionary Force from the beaches of Dunkirk on the English Channel got underway. Everything that would float—boats, ships, fishing vessels, and yachts—was pressed into service.

Tuesday
27

1919—The U.S. Navy seaplane NC-4 landed in Lisbon, Portugal, the first aircraft to fly across the Atlantic Ocean.

Wednesday
28

1921—The whaleship *Charles W. Morgan*, whose whaling career began in 1841, returned to Provincetown, Massachusetts, at the end of her last voyage.

Thursday
29

1930—Frank Cowper, author of *Cruising Sails and Yachting Tales*, as well as *Sailing Tours*, an early five-volume cruising guide to the British Isles, died in Winchester, Hampshire, England.

Friday
30

1866—Three tea clippers—*Ariel*, *Taeping*, and *Serica*—departed Foochow, China, on the same tide; they would dock in London, England, on the same tide, September 5.

Saturday
31

1983—Jack Dempsey, U.S. Coast Guard veteran and heavyweight boxing champion of the world, died in New York City.

Sunday
1

1947—USS *Sea Robin* (SS-407) became the first submarine to round Cape Horn.

NATURAL FIBER ROPE, LATE 19TH CENTURY

Name	Made From	Lay
Yarn	Fiber	Right-handed
Strand	Yarns	Left- or right-handed
Hawser laid	3 strands	Opposite to the strands
Shroud laid	4 strands and a heart	Right-handed
Cable laid	3 hawser-laid ropes	Left-handed
Spunyarn	3 to 9 yarns	Right-handed
Sennit	Yarns	Plaited
Nettle stuff	2 or 3 left-handed yarns	Right-handed
Fox	Short yarns laid up by hand	Left-handed

Running rigging was hawser laid, right-handed.
Gun gear was hawser laid, left-handed.
Standing rigging was shroud laid.

OTHER TYPES OF ROPE

Twine—small stuff made from the finest hemp

Coir rope—made from coconut fibers; used for warps, as it floats

Hide rope—made from rawhide; stronger than hemp rope, but had to be kept dry and well greased as it would swell when wet; used for wheel ropes

Junk—made from condemned hemp rope, pulled apart; for seizing stuff, spunyarn, sennit, mats, swabs, etc.

Rounding—made from smaller condemned rope; for wads, etc.

Oakum—made from yarns picked from old hemp rope; for caulking

In that building, long and low,
With its windows all a-row,
Like the port-holes of a hulk
Human spiders spin and spin,
Backward down their threads so thin
Dropping, each a hempen bulk.

—from "The Ropewalk"
by Henry Wadsworth Longfellow

THE 21-FOOT KETCH *KATE*, LONDON, ENGLAND, JUNE 5, 1869

Everything was in readiness to haul out into the river at tide time. There was little or no water to float the boat out into the river, but mud abounded to such a depth as required the combined power of about thirty men to drag the little boat into the stream; giving me a very satisfactory test of the strength of my rope cable, and rendering it serviceable by a good stretching. Everything was in readiness for a start by 7 p.m. The wind had been strong and puffy throughout the day; but who could possibly give the weather a thought when possessed of a brand new boat, brand new sails, rigging, flags, and experience?

—E.E. Middleton

There is no end to the sky and the waters.
　　　　　　　　　　—Albert Camus

JUNE

Monday
2

1877—Officers of the British royal yacht *Osborne* sighted a sea serpent off the coast of Sicily.

Tuesday
3

1967—Arthur Ransome, author of *Racundra's First Cruise* and the *Swallows and Amazons* series, died in Manchester, England.

Wednesday
4

1833—The ship-rigged Baltimore clipper *Ann McKim*, considered by historians to be either the ultimate refinement of the Baltimore clipper model or the first of the clipper ships, was launched in Baltimore, Maryland.

Thursday
5

1988—Australian singlehander Kay Cottee returned to Sydney in the 37-foot yacht *Blackmores First Lady*, the first woman to accomplish a nonstop circumnavigation of the globe.

Friday
6

1977—A fishing boat capsized during a severe thunderstorm near the Chesapeake Bay Bridge Tunnel with the loss of 13 of the 27 persons on board; winds approaching 100 mph were recorded in Norfolk, Virginia.

Saturday
7

1867—An international congress to consider the future of the salmon fishery convened in South Kensington, London, England.

Sunday
8

1787—The full-rigged ship *Bethia*, built in 1783, was renamed HMS *Bounty*.

A FEW ARTISTS WHOSE MARINE SUBJECTS EXHIBIT BOTH TECHNICAL ACCURACY AND "HEART"

George Bellows
Arthur Briscoe
John Constable
E.W. Cooke
Fred S. Cozzens
Montague Dawson
William Gilkerson
Gordon Grant
Winslow Homer
Edward Hopper
Rockwell Kent
Fitz Hugh Lane
Robert Salmon
Warren Sheppard
Arthur Spurling
J.M.W. Turner
Willem van de Velde, the Elder and the Younger
W.L. Wyllie

ON THE REPRESENTATION OF SHIPS, I

I wonder why in pictures of vessels at sea they are almost always represented as under full sail, with a fair breeze. In reality they should be represented close-hauled in a gale of wind, beating up for port against a head sea.
—Thomas Gibson Bowles

ON THE REPRESENTATION OF SHIPS, II

Too many popular ship paintings are idealistic and romantic: the "blue water school," with snowy white sails and sunlight dancing on the waves. Although these images are undeniably attractive, the reality was usually rather different.   —Vice-Admiral Sir Patrick Bayly

ON THE IMMORTAL LIGHT OF THE SEA

The light you get at sea never fades. It is not only revealing; it has a suggestion of imperishable origin. You bring a reflection of it ashore with you, without knowing it.
—H.M. Tomlinson

ON GIVING CREDIT WHERE CREDIT IS DUE

I remember being handed a score composed by Mozart at the age of eleven. What could I say? I felt like de Kooning, who was asked to comment on a certain abstract painting, and answered in the negative. He was then told it was the work of a celebrated monkey. "That's different. For a monkey, it's terrific."
—Igor Stravinsky

THE CONVERTED LIFEBOAT *FALCON*, ZUIDER ZEE, NETHERLANDS, JUNE 15, 1886

What small amount of wind there was came right aft, and we contrived, to the gratification of our pride, to run away from all the schuyts. As we came out of the estuary of the Y, the view of the Zuider Zee was a singular one. The heat had produced a thin haze, which did not obscure but surrounded objects with a golden atmosphere. Seawards only the horizon was not visible; there the sky and water mingled in a beautiful sunlit mist that Turner would have loved to paint, while distant fishing-vessels seemed to be floating in the air. Along the shore we were following, stretched as far as the eye could see the massive grass-grown dyke; above which rose here and there red roof-tops, steeples, and trees. Farther still a tall church-spire stood out of the waters, like an island; the low land round it being beneath the horizon; this, from its bearings, I took to be the church at Hoorn.
—E.F. Knight

Of all the works of the Creation none is so imposing as the Ocean.
—John Constable

JUNE

Monday
9

1984—Amyr Khan Klink of Brazil got underway from Bahia de Lüderitz, Namibia, on a solo row across the South Atlantic Ocean to Praia di Espera, Brazil.

Tuesday
10

1896—Congress authorized the establishment of the first experimental ship-model tank in the United States.

Wednesday
11

1910—Jacques-Yves Cousteau, underwater documentarian and co-inventor of the Aqua-Lung, was born in St.-André-de-Cubzac, France.

Thursday
12

1867—The sailing pontoon raft *Nonpareil*, built by the Monitor Life-saving Raft Company, got underway from New York for England; she arrived there in late July.

Friday
13

1917—The U.S. Coast Guard cutter *McCulloch* sank in a collision with a steamship off Point Conception, California.

Saturday
14 FLAG DAY

Sunday
15 FATHER'S DAY

We heard her a mile to west'ard—the liner that
   cut us through—
As crushing the fog at a twenty-jog she drove with
   her double screw.
We heard her a mile to west'ard as she bellowed
   to clear her path,
The grum, grim grunt of her whistle, a leviathan's
   growl of wrath.
We could tell she was aimed to smash us, so we
   clashed at our little bell,
But the sound was shredded by screaming wind
   and we simply rung our knell.
And the feeble breath, that screamed at Death
   through our horn, was beaten back,
And we knew that doom rode up the sea toward
   the shell of our tossing smack.
                              —Holman F. Day

WHAT TO DO IF YOU ARE SUDDENLY BESET BY FOG

   Immediately mark the time and your position on the chart.
   Get out your fog-signaling device and start using it.
   If close to shore, turn on your depth sounder or get out your leadline or sounding pole.
   Assign a bow lookout.

ASSUMPTIONS ABOUT SOUND SIGNALS IN THE FOG THAT *NEVER SHOULD BE MADE:*

   Because a sound signal cannot be heard, its source is out of hearing range.
   Because a signal sounds a long way off, it is.
   Because a signal sounds close, it is.
   Because a signal is audible during one set of circumstances, it will always be audible in the same set of circumstances.
   Because a signal that you know to be nearby is not heard, it is not sounding.
   Because a signal sounds as if it is coming from a particular direction, it is.

THE DEVELOPMENT OF THE LAND-BASED FOG SIGNAL

   Early 18th century—bell rung by hand
   1719—signal cannon installed at the Boston Harbor Light, Massachusetts
   Mid-19th century—bell rung mechanically
   Mid-19th century—compressed-air trumpet
   1854—bell buoy
   Late 1850s—steam whistle
   1866—reed horn
   1866—siren
   1876—whistling buoy

THE 30-FOOT CUTTER *EMANUEL*, NORTH ATLANTIC, EAST OF NEWFOUNDLAND, JUNE 17, 1934

   Another day of calm and also of fog. Now that my port was not far off, the enforced delay and inaction were very irksome. For days I had seemed to be living in a little world of my own only about 500 yards across. During the morning my sense of isolation was suddenly broken by the sound of a steamer's syren. I jumped below to get my fog-horn, and replied with three short blasts, the signal for a ship running before the wind, though, in fact, the yacht had barely steerage way. It is not likely that the puny squeak of my instrument was heard on board the steamer. For a time the noise of her syren increased; then it gradually died away, and my world contracted to its original isolation. The steamer never came into view.
                              —Commander R.D. Graham

Fog upsets all reckonings.
—Rockwell Kent

JUNE

Monday
16

1927—USS *Constitution*, "Old Ironsides," was drydocked in Boston, Massachusetts, for restoration.

Tuesday
17

1802—The American merchant brig *Franklin* was captured by Tripolitan pirates in the Mediterranean, an act, in combination with others, that eventually led to war.

Wednesday
18

1875—An intense storm, now thought to have been an early-season hurricane, struck the coast of New England, bringing high winds, heavy surf, and considerable damage to shipping.

Thursday
19

1852—The great clipper ship *Sovereign of the Seas* was launched from the Donald McKay shipyard, East Boston, Massachusetts.

Friday
20

1872—The flying start was used for the first time in a yacht race sponsored by the New York Yacht Club.

Saturday
21 SUMMER SOLSTICE

Sunday
22

1978—Karen Hansen became the first woman to graduate from the Webb Institute of Naval Architecture, Glen Cove, New York.

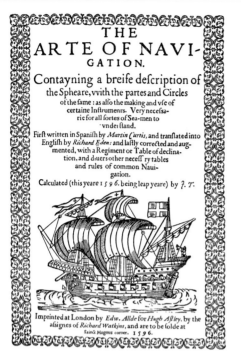

MINIMUM NAVIGATIONAL TOOLS
Piloting, small boats
- Accurate compass whose deviation is known
- Up-to-date chart
- Parallel rules, dividers, pencil, and eraser
- Common sense
- Electronic aid: GPS

Piloting, yachts
- Compass
- Pelorus
- Charts
- Plotting equipment
- Means for measuring speed or distance
- Logbook
- Tide and tidal current tables
- Light list
- Coast pilot or sailing directions
- Hand lead
- Binoculars
- Flashlight
- Stopwatch
- Fog signal apparatus
- Barometer
- Thermometer
- Electronic aids: radar, GPS, depth sounder

Offshore work
- All of the above, plus:
- Sextant
- Accurate timepiece
- Almanac
- Sight reduction tables
- Star finder
- Electronic aids: radar, GPS, depth sounder

THE SHIP'S LIBRARY OF THE *SPRAY* DURING JOSHUA SLOCUM'S SINGLEHANDED VOYAGE AROUND THE WORLD
The Descent of Man and *The Expression of the Emotions in Man and Animals*, Darwin
Popular Astronomy, Newcomb
Total Eclipses of the Sun, Todd
The Naturalist on the Amazons, Bates
History of England, Macaulay
Life of Macaulay, Trevelyan
Life of Columbus, Irving
Life of Johnson, Boswell
Don Quixote, Cervantes
Life on the Mississippi, Twain
Several books by Robert Louis Stevenson
A complete set of Shakespeare's plays
Books of poetry by Lamb, Moore, Burns, Tennyson, and Longfellow

THE PRINCIPAL METHODS OF NAVIGATION
Piloting—fixing position within sight of land or aids to navigation; aka coastal navigation

Celestial—fixing position by reference to the sun, the moon, various planets, and various stars

Dead (deduced, or ded.) reckoning—determining approximate position by plotting courses and distances from the last positive position determined by either piloting or celestial navigation

Electronic—fixing position by such electronic devices as radar, GPS, and others

THE OYSTER SLOOP *SPRAY*, NORTH OF AUSTRALIA, JUNE 27, 1897
For several days now the *Spray* sailed west on the parallel of 10 degrees 25′ S., as true as a hair. If she deviated at all from that, through the day or night,—and this may have happened,—she was back, strangely enough, at noon, at the same latitude. But the greatest science was in reckoning the longitude. My tin clock and only timepiece had by this time lost its minute-hand, but after I boiled her she told the hours, and that was near enough on a long stretch.

—Joshua Slocum

I have met poor grammarians who were good navigators, but I have never met a good navigator who was not an exceptionally intelligent man.
—Felix Riesenberg

JUNE

Monday 23

1716—The Province of Massachusetts authorized the construction of the first lighthouse in North America, on Great Brewster Island, Boston Harbor.

Tuesday 24

It is sad to think of the lost art of the sea, that art of the fid and marlinspike, of the log-chip and the lead-line.
—Basil Lubboc

Wednesday 25

1901—A contract was signed for the construction of the first and only seven-masted schooner, the *Thomas W. Lawson*.

Thursday 26

1803—The coppering of the bottom of the U.S. frigate *Constitution*—with plates made by Paul Revere—was completed in Boston, Massachusetts.

Friday 27

1942—The FBI announced that eight German saboteurs had landed from a submarine on Long Island, New York, and had been captured.

Saturday 28

1976—The first women, 38 in all, were enrolled in the U.S. Coast Guard Academy.

Sunday 29

1812—The Baltimore clipper *Nonsuch* was awarded privateer Commission no. 1 for service in the War of 1812.

WORDS TO THE WISE CONCERNING SMALL-BOAT CRUISING FROM DIXON KEMP

Should the cruise be intended to extend over a couple of weeks, in localities where shops are never heard of, an extra supply of everything should be taken, but not so much as to have a superfluity of any one thing. It is a well-known fact that the oftener one goes cruising, the fewer unnecessaries are taken.

You should not try to lug along what you are trying to leave behind. —L. Francis Herreshoff

HOMEMADE BRASS CLEANER AND POLISH

1 cup vinegar   1 cup salt   ¼ cup flour

Mix into paste, apply to brass, allow to dry, wipe off with clean, soft rag.

CLEANER AND POLISH FOR DEEPLY TARNISHED BRASS

3 parts water   1 part muriatic acid

Mix together, apply to surface, rinse thoroughly. Rub down with a cloth soaked in Worcestershire sauce.

PROTECTION FOR SHINED BRASS

At sea—buff the surface with automobile paste wax or any other wax rated for exterior use.

For winter storage—coat with Vaseline, light machine oil, or WD-40.

THE CONVERTED MOTOR LIFEBOAT *ETERNAL WAVE*, NORWEGIAN COAST, JULY 1, 1933

We proceeded Northward to Balholm, getting away a little before intended as there was disturbance by trading boats coming alongside, and when clear we let *Eternal Wave* drift during breakfast. Then we passed, in a wide open part of the fjord, many fishing boats working seine nets for the Norwegian sardine fishery. After a walk ashore at Balholm we continued up the fjord—the wind S.W. fresh and still overcast with cloud on the mountains—and then turned Southerly into and through the 15 miles of the dark and narrow Naero Fjord, its precipitous mountain sides rising high above, and at 1824 made fast alongside the quay at Gudvangen intending to remain there for the week-end. But there was depression in the shut-in location, deep under the overpowering mountains, and we would leave.

—T.N. Dinwiddy

At sea I learned how little a person needs, not how much.
—Robin Lee Graham

JUNE/JULY

Monday
30

1973—Maurice and Maralyn Bailey, who had taken to a life raft and drifted for 118 days after their 28-foot yacht *Auralyn* was rammed and sunk by whales northeast of the Galápagos Islands, were rescued by a fishing vessel.

Tuesday
1 CANADA DAY

1993—Tom McNally arrived in Fort Lauderdale, Florida, at the end of a record transatlantic passage in the smallest boat to date, the 5-foot-11-inch sailboat *Vera Hugh, Pride of Liverpool.*

Wednesday
2

1843—An alligator was reported to have fallen out of the sky during a thunderstorm accompanied by strong winds in the port city of Charleston, South Carolina.

Thursday
3

The traditional beginning of summer's "Dog Days," named after Sirius, the Dog Star, which rises in the east with the sun at this time of year.

Friday
4 INDEPENDENCE DAY

1833—The Royal Yacht Club, founded in London in 1815 as The Yacht Club, was renamed the Royal Yacht Squadron.

Saturday
5

1884—The Bureau of Navigation, charged with the administration of the navigation laws, was established by an Act of Congress.

Sunday
6

There is a wonderful deal of romance in sailing lists, and advertisements of ships for sale—and in charts.   —C. Fox Smith

WEATHER PORTENTS, ACCORDING TO A. HYATT VERRILL

Unusual twinkling of stars; double horns to the moon; halos around stars or moon; "wind dogs"—increasing wind, or rain with a liability of wind

Wind shifting from west to east—increase of wind from the other direction

Rosy sky at sunset—fine weather

Sickly, greenish-colored sunset—wind and rain

Dark red or crimson sunset—rain

Bright-yellow sky at sunset—wind

Pale-yellow, or saffron, sunset—rain

Mixed red and yellow sunset—rain and squally weather

Remarkably clear atmosphere with distant objects standing above the water and seemingly in air—wind, usually from the northwest, and often rain

Heavy dews—fine weather

Fogs—change in weather and little wind

Misty clouds on hills, remaining stationary, increasing or descending—rain and wind

Misty clouds on hills, rising or dispersing—fairer weather

Red morning sky—bad weather and wind

Gray morning sky—fine weather

High dawn (dawn seen above a bank of clouds)—wind

Low dawn (daylight breaking close to the horizon)—fair

Soft, delicate clouds—fair and light winds

Hard-edged, oily clouds—wind

Dark, gloomy sky—windy

Light, bright sky—fine weather

Small, inky clouds—rain

Light "scud," or small clouds moving across heavier clouds—wind and rain

Light, scudding clouds by themselves—wind and dry weather

High, upper clouds scudding past moon or stars in a different direction from the lower cloud-masses—change of wind

Fine weather followed by light streaks, wisps, or mottled patches of distant clouds that increase and join—change

Haze that becomes murky and clouds the sky—change to bad weather

Light, delicate colors, with soft-edged clouds—fine weather

Brilliant, or gaudy, colors and sharp, hard-edged clouds—rain and wind

Mackerel sky (small, separate, white clouds covering the sky)—wet weather

"Mares' tails" (long, wispy, curved, isolated clouds against a blue sky)—wind

Rainbow early in the morning—bad weather

Rainbow in afternoon—fair

THE CUTTER *ESPAÑOLA*, WEST COAST OF SCOTLAND, JULY 7, 1921

I held on with as stout a heart as I could command in the clammy obscurity, seeing nothing beyond the bowsprit end. It is a situation of this kind which makes one wonder why we voluntarily devote our annual month of holidays to such foolishness. After an hour of anxious suspense I was suddenly aware of a flaw in the dead curtain of fog. A thin vertical column of light appeared ahead, and did not disappear. Quickly it defined itself, unmistakably, as a small white tower. In thirty seconds we knew we were actually looking at the Guilean Beacon. It was like winning an enormous prize in a State lottery. I still have on the chart the pencil track I drew when laying the course, but I am as incapable of explaining how I did it with such accuracy as Einstein is of demonstrating his famous prediction. —H.M. Wright

*Seagull, seagull, get out on t'sand,
We'll ne'er have good weather with thee on t'land.*
—old weather saying

JULY

Monday
7

1952—Stanley Sayres, driving the raceboat *Slo-Mo-Shun*, set a world propeller-driven water speed record to date of 178.497 mph, on Lake Washington, Seattle, Washington.

Tuesday
8

1875—The crew of the sailing ship *Pauline*, with a cargo of coal, off Cabo de São Roque, Brazil, observed what is thought to have been a giant squid attacking a sperm whale.

Wednesday
9

1865—John MacGregor, the inventor of the Rob Roy canoe, set out on his first canoe voyage, a modest trip on the River Thames, England.

Thursday
10

1915—The pilot schooner *New Jersey* was run down and sunk off the coast of New York by the United Fruit steamer *Marchioneal*.

Friday
11

1955—The wreck of the Union ironclad *Monitor*, sunk in a gale off Cape Hatteras in 1862, was discovered by Robert F. Marx.

Saturday
12 BANK HOLIDAY / UK & N. IRELAND

Sunday
13

1851—The clipper ship *Challenge*, largest of the type to date, got underway on her maiden voyage from New York to San Francisco.

Tacking

TECHNICAL SEA TERMS LIKELY TO BE ENCOUNTERED IN HISTORICAL READING

Weather side—the side against which the wind blows

Lee side—the opposite to the weather side

To weather—to pass on the weather side of anything

Tack—go from one tack to another with the bow passing through the wind

Wear—go from one tack to another with the stern passing through the wind

Beat—sail as close into the wind as possible by continually tacking

Close-hauled; aka on the wind, by the wind—sailing as close to the wind as possible

Off the wind—sailing with the wind on the beam or quarter

By the lee—the vessel is running, but with the wind blowing from the same quarter as the boom is lying

Full-and-bye—sailing almost close-hauled, with all sails filled and pulling strongly

Before the wind—sailing downwind

Reach—the wind is blowing more or less on the vessel's beam

Beam reach—the wind is directly on the vessel's beam

Broad reach—the wind is blowing on the vessel's quarter

Make a sternboard, or make stern way—go astern

Make lee way—go sideways, away from the wind

Scud—sail downwind before a strong wind or gale

Haul the wind—steer as nearly into the wind as possible

Heave to—allow the sails to cancel each other out, thus keeping the ship stationary

Lie to—in a gale set only enough sail to keep the ship's head to the wind

In stays—headed directly into the wind, with steerageway

In irons—headed directly into the wind, without steerageway

Luffing—the sails are not completely filled with wind

Weather tide—a tidal current that carries a vessel toward the wind

Lee tide—a tidal current that carries a vessel away from the wind

THE AMERICAN MERCHANT BRIG *SALLY & MARY*, NORTH ATLANTIC, JULY 17, 1812

I had just entered upon the eastern edge of the grand Bank. At day light, I went on deck; we had a light breeze of wind from the north, with all sails sett, that would draw, in casting my Eye to windward, I saw a sail, to appearance, bearing down directly for us—not having spoken any thing, I told the mate, to back the main yard & would speak her, we accordingly did; & at sunrise I ordered the Insign hoisted, at the Mizen peak; no sooner were our colours up, than his went up in the smoke of a gun, I saw that she was a Schooner, under English colours, & that she was armed.... —Captain Elijah Cobb

BY YOUR LANGUAGE SHALL YOU BE KNOWN, SAYS CARL LANE

Those who make no attempt to learn the language are not only almost inarticulate among more seasoned skippers but are sometimes quite ridiculous. A tiller, we must remember, can never be a steering stick nor can a sheet be a sail or a cleat be a thingamajig or below be downstairs.

To have a good vacation—Never Beat.
            —old saying

JULY

Monday
14

1952—The new passenger liner SS *United States* set a record to date for a westbound crossing of the Atlantic Ocean of 3 days, 12 hours, and 12 minutes.

Tuesday
15

1883—A Mr. Terry arrived in Paris, France, aboard a boat built over the framework of a tricycle; he had pedaled from London, England, to Dover, across the English Channel to Calais, and thence overland to Paris.

Wednesday
16

1915—The battleships *Ohio*, *Missouri*, and *Wisconsin* became the first ships of the U.S. Navy to pass through the Panama Canal.

Thursday
17

1812—The U.S. frigate *Constitution* successfully eluded a British squadron after a three-day chase, much of it in light air, off the coast of New Jersey.

Friday
18

1792—John Paul Jones, U.S. naval hero, victor in the battle between the *Bonhomme Richard* and HMS *Serapis*, died in Paris, France.

Saturday
19

1843—I.K. Brunel's steamship *Great Britain*, the first vessel with a screw propeller to cross the Atlantic, was launched in Bristol, England.

Sunday
20

1876—The 141-foot extreme centerboard schooner *Mohawk* capsized and sank during a squall in New York Harbor.

PROS AND CONS OF THE POPULAR CRUISING-YACHT RIGS

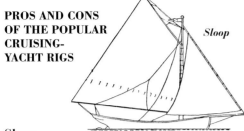
Sloop

Sloop
One mast, at least two sails (main and jib).

Pro—Only two primary sails to handle; mast stepped relatively far forward, allowing more open space in the saloon (assuming the mast is stepped on the keel); rigging relatively simple.

Con—Forward-stepped mast concentrates weight toward bow, sometimes causing the hull to plunge into steep seas; heaving-to without a split foretriangle can be problematic in some conditions; relatively large size of the mainsail can cause difficulty in handling, especially when reefing.

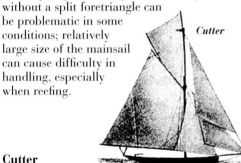
Cutter

Cutter
One mast, at least three sails (main, forestaysail, jib).

Pro—Good balance between the headsails and the mainsail; more possible sail combinations than the sloop; heaving-to relatively easy.

Con—Relatively large mainsail can be difficult to handle; position of the mast when stepped on the keel breaks up the open space in the saloon; more rigging required than the sloop.

Yawl

Ketch

Yawl and Ketch
Yawl: *Two masts, at least three sails (main, jib, mizzen), the after mast stepped behind the rudderpost.*
Ketch: *Two masts, at least three sails (main, jib, mizzen), the after mast stepped forward of the rudderpost.*

Pro—Large after-sail triangle broken up into a smaller main and small mizzen; more reduced-sail combinations possible; mainmast stepped farther forward than the cutter, preserving open space below.

Con—Windward ability not as good as the cutter's, nor is it as fast, size for size; more spars and rigging required than for the sloop and the cutter.

Schooner

Schooner
Two or more masts, at least three sails (main, fore, jib), the forward mast shorter than the after one, or of equal height.

Pro—Many possible sail combinations; fast off the wind; handsome.

Con—Largish mainsail; complex rigging; can be difficult to handle with a shorthanded crew.

THE BARK *CORIOLANUS*, ATLANTIC OCEAN, BOUND FOR THE CAPE VERDE ISLANDS, JULY 21, 1929

The chronometer tings five times. In a minute it is loudly echoed aft and forward, the man at the wheel giving a flippant rhythm to his banging, the lookout answering with a touch of his own personality. "Gong, clangety clang gong!"

It was raining, the wind S.E., the ship going languidly before it. Later when the sun came hot, the wind died. For three hours we drifted, the water very blue and calm, but sometimes curving, skin-smooth, over a moving hill. The deck dips slowly; the wave crashes into gleaming foam along our entire length. Then calmly, steadily again. In the afternoon the breeze returned from the same quarter.
—Norman Matson

The rhythm of waves beats in the sea like a pulse in living flesh.
—Henry Beston

JULY

Monday
21

1997—The USS *Constitution*, in celebration of her bicentennial, got underway under sail for the first time in 116 years, off Marblehead, Massachusetts.

Tuesday
22

1957—Singlehander Wolfgang Kraker von Schwarzenfeld took to his inflatable dinghy after his trimaran capsized in the Atlantic 1,200 miles east of New York; 18 days later, he was rescued by a passing ship.

Wednesday
23

1883—A pier in North Point, Baltimore, Maryland, gave way, drowning approximately 65 excursionists.

Thursday
24

1965—All U.S. Navy icebreakers were turned over to the U.S. Coast Guard.

Friday
25

1943—The first ship in the U.S. Navy named for an African-American, the destroyer escort USS *Harmon*, was launched.

Saturday
26

1956—Egypt seized the Suez Canal.

Sunday
27

1852—The steamboat *Henry Clay* burned on the Hudson River, New York; more than 70 lives were lost.

THE CLIPPER SHIP *FLYING CLOUD*, PACIFIC OCEAN, WEST OF CHILE, JULY 31, 1851

Lat. 36.58 Lon. 95.46 SE Fresh breezes fine weather 2 PM wind SE, at 6 squally, In lower & topgallant studdingsails at 7 in Royals, at 2 AM in Fore topmast studding-sail, Latter part High sea running ship very wet, fore & aft, Distance Run this Day by observation 374 miles, an average of 15 7/12 knots per hour, during the Squalls 18 knots of line was not sufficient to measure her rate of speed.
—Captain Josiah P. Cressy

MARCH OF THE RECORD FOR NAUTICAL MILES RUN IN 24 HOURS BY A SAILING YACHT

1984, *Crédit Agricole*, catamaran
508.6 (21.19 knots, avg.)
1990, *Jet Services*, catamaran
522.7 (21.78 knots, avg.)
1994, *Primagaz*, trimaran
540 (22.5 knots, avg.)
1999, *Playstation*, catamaran
580 (24.17 knots, avg.)
2001, *Playstation*, catamaran
687.17 (28.63 knots, avg.)

All these are multihulls. The best distance run in 24 hours by a monohull was 467.7 nautical miles (19.49 knots, avg.) by *Armor Lux—Foie Gras Bizac* in 2001.

By contrast, any of the mid-19th-century clipper ships, if they could be resurrected (with their skippers and crews), would still be competitive with today's best multihull and monohull yachts. The clipper-ship record of 465 miles was set on December 12, 1854, by Champion of the Seas in the Southern Ocean between Africa and Australia—quite an achievement for a commercial vessel.

MARCH OF THE RECORD FOR SAILING AROUND THE WORLD NONSTOP IN A CREWED YACHT

1993–94, *Explorer*, catamaran
79 days, 6 hours, 15 minutes, 56 seconds; average speed 11.35 knots
1994–95, *Enza*, catamaran
74 days, 22 hours, 17 minutes, 22 seconds; average speed 12 knots
1997, *Sport Elec*, trimaran
71 days, 14 hours, 22 minutes, 8 seconds; average speed 12.66 knots
2000–01, *Innovation Explorer*, catamaran
64 days, 22 hours, 32 minutes; average speed 18.45 knots

By contrast, the first person to sail alone around the world nonstop was Robin Knox-Johnston in the ketch *Suhaili*, 312 days (1968–69); average speed 3.6 knots.

KEEP THIS IN MIND WHEN CONSIDERING SPEED RECORDS, SAYS HOWARD I. CHAPELLE

Speed under sail has commonly been judged solely by "record passages" between ports and by record "day's runs." These take no account of the difference in the size of the competing ships, nor of their loadings. Record passages were sometimes made when the fastest hour's run was at a relatively low speed. Such passages were often accountable to exceptionally favorable wind and weather and to good command, rather than to good ship design.

There are few sports so extremely elastic in their financial aspect as yachting.
— Francis B. Cooke

JULY/AUG

Monday
28

1866—An Act of Congress authorized the Secretary of the Treasury to devise a numbering system for vessels of the United States, the numbers to be carved or otherwise permanently marked on the main beam.

Tuesday
29

The ocean knows no favorites.
— Samuel Eliot Morison

Wednesday
30

1844—The New York Yacht Club, the first in the United States, was established aboard the yacht *Gimcrack* off the Battery, New York Harbor.

Thursday
31

1715—Eleven Spanish treasure ships carrying nearly seven million pieces of eight were struck by a hurricane off Florida and driven onto shoals; all the ships and approximately 1,200 lives were lost.

Friday
1

1897—George Harbo and Frank Samuelson, the first to row intentionally across an ocean, arrived in St. Mary's, Scilly Isles, from New York in the 18-foot open pulling boat *Fox*.

Saturday
2

1844—The first annual cruise of the New York Yacht Club got underway, destination Newport, Rhode Island.

Sunday
3

1942—Mildred McAfee became the first woman to receive an officer's commission in the U.S. naval forces.

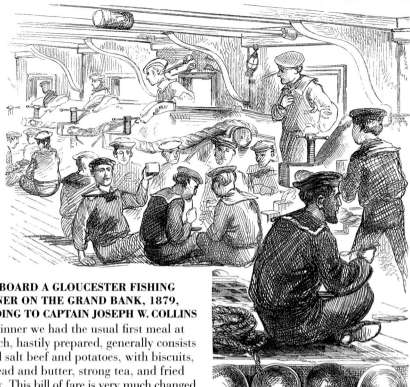

GRUB ABOARD A GLOUCESTER FISHING SCHOONER ON THE GRAND BANK, 1879, ACCORDING TO CAPTAIN JOSEPH W. COLLINS

For dinner we had the usual first meal at sea, which, hastily prepared, generally consists of boiled salt beef and potatoes, with biscuits, pilot-bread and butter, strong tea, and fried beefsteak. This bill of fare is very much changed as soon as the cook has time to prepare a greater variety, and, though beefsteak or other fresh meat is rarely seen after the first few days out, the table is well provided with plenty of good raised bread, cakes, pies, duff, etc., and last, though not least, the finest fish are served up in a manner rarely equaled elsewhere.

THE BARK *JOHN ENA*, MID-ATLANTIC OCEAN, NEAR THE EQUATOR, AUGUST 4, 1911

Right now our food and water are considerably below par. We have more salt fish and less bully beef these days, and potatoes in small quantity about once every third or fourth day. The starboard watch brought up a new cask of beef today, but apparently the cooperage had been sprung, permitting air to get inside the cask, as the beef was so rotten it stunk to high Heaven. I have never smelled anything so sickening. It was awful, and all hands heaved sighs of relief when the cask was put over the side and sank out of sight. The nauseating stench, however, hung around the ship for hours. That means still more pickled or salt fish from now on.
—C. Ray Wilmore

LET'S HEAR IT FOR CLAM CHOWDER

Mrs. Hussey...said—"Clam or Cod?"

"What's that about Cods, ma'am?" said I, with much politeness.

"Clam or Cod?" she repeated.

"A clam for supper? A cold clam; is THAT what you mean, Mrs. Hussey?" says I, "but that's a rather cold and clammy reception in the winter time, ain't it, Mrs. Hussey?"...

Mrs. Hussey hurried towards an open door leading to the kitchen, and bawling out "clam for two," disappeared.

"Queequeg," said I, "do you think that we can make out a supper for us both on one clam?"

However, a warm savory steam from the kitchen served to belie the apparently cheerless prospect before us. But when that smoking chowder came in, the mystery was delightfully explained. Oh, sweet friends! hearken to me. It was made of small juicy clams, scarcely bigger than hazel nuts, mixed with pounded ship biscuit, and salted pork cut up into little flakes; the whole enriched with butter, and plentifully seasoned with pepper and salt.
—from *Moby-Dick*, by Herman Melville

To me, nothing made by man is more beautiful than a sailboat under way in fine weather.
—Robert Manry

AUGUST

Monday
4
CIVIC HOLIDAY / CANADA
SUMMMER BANK HOLIDAY / SCOTLAND

1852—The clipper ship *Sovereign of the Seas*, the largest merchant sailing ship in the world at the time, got underway on her maiden voyage, from New York to San Francisco.

Tuesday
5

1889—For the first time, uniforms were required, and prescribed, for keepers and surfmen of the U.S. Life-Saving Service.

Wednesday
6

1918—The Diamond Shoals Lightship was sunk by a German submarine; the crew took to their boats and survived.

Thursday
7

1789—The Lighthouse Establishment, a division of the Treasury Department, later known as the Lighthouse Service, eventually part of the U.S. Coast Guard, was founded by an Act of Congress.

Friday
8

1972—For the first time, women of the U.S. Navy were authorized for sea duty as part of the regular ship's company.

Saturday
9

1841—The steamboat *Erie* burned on Lake Erie with the loss of 180 lives.

Sunday
10

1860—The Buffalo Yacht Club, one of the oldest in the United States, was founded in Buffalo, New York.

THE SEQUENCE OF A TIDAL CURRENT
Flood
Maximum flood
Slack
Ebb begins
Ebb
Maximum ebb
Slack
Flood begins
Etc.

FACTORS AFFECTING TIDAL CURRENTS

Shoals, reefs, sandbars, submerged obstructions, headlands, channels, and river mouths can affect tidal currents.

In straight channels and tidal rivers, the strongest currents are usually in the middle.

In curved channels, the strongest currents and deepest water are usually near the outer edge of the curve.

Countercurrents and eddies can occur on either side of a channel, especially around obstructions and near bights.

Tidal currents usually reach their greatest velocity in a narrow passage connecting two large bodies of water.

Tide rips—extremely turbulent water in a tidal current—are caused by an irregular bottom, or by a sharp change in the depth of the water, such as at the edges of banks or reefs.

Vessels are sometimes retarded, and sometimes forwarded in their voyages, by currents at sea, which are not often perceived.
—Benjamin Franklin

THE EFFECT OF TIDAL CURRENTS

A tidal current that is directly against you will slow your speed but not affect your course.

A tidal current that is running directly with your course will increase your speed but not affect your course.

A tidal current that is neither directly against you nor with you will affect your course and speed to a greater or lesser extent, depending on the angle of your course to it.

THE KETCH *MARSAILIDH*, CHANNEL ISLANDS, AUGUST 16, 1921

2 p.m.—Tacked and stood W. by N. for Creux harbour, Sark, as the ebb was nearly finished, and it meant a long beat over a foul tide to make Guernsey. At 3 p.m., about ½ mile E. of Creux, we sailed quite suddenly out of a weak fair tide into a strong northerly set, at the same time losing what little wind we had, dropped the second anchor with 30 fathoms of chain in 12 fathoms sand. A motor fishing boat came off and offered to tow us in, which we accepted. She attempted the Goulet, but another boat had to come and help her owing to the strength of the tide which boiled over the rocks like a salmon stream. Moored to the north wall at 5 p.m., and grounded on the ebb.
—J.F.N. Baxendale

If there is any pleasure greater than that of steering a smart little yacht to windward in a fresh breeze, I have never experienced it.
—Francis B. Cooke

AUGUST

Monday
11

The traditional end of summer's "Dog Days," named after Sirius, the Dog Star.

Tuesday ○
12

1914—John Philip Holland, the inventor of the modern submarine, died in Newark, New Jersey.

Wednesday
13

1984—The 36-foot cruising yacht *Eumel* sailed herself aground near Kronsgard, Denmark; her singlehanded skipper, Werner Jacob, had disappeared and was never found.

Thursday
14

1873—The weekly journal *Forest and Stream*, with regular coverage of the yachting and boating scene, began publication.

Friday
15

1865—Although the Suez Canal would not be officially opened for another four years, the first vessel under her own power, a coal carrier, made the passage from the Mediterranean to the Red Sea.

Saturday
16

1787—Lieutenant William Bligh, Royal Navy, was appointed commander of HMS *Bounty*.

Sunday
17

1879—A wind speed of 138 mph was recorded during a hurricane at Cape Lookout, North Carolina.

WHEN CHOOSING AN ANCHOR, CONSIDER THESE FACTORS

Is it suitable for the bottom conditions—mud, sand, rock, weed, etc.—of your expected cruising grounds?

Does it have enough holding power to handle your boat in the worst conditions?

How easy is it to stow and to use? If it is a folding or take-apart anchor, how difficult is it to make ready for use?

How likely is it to foul?

Can it be recovered easily?

USE OF A DRIFT LEAD WHEN AT ANCHOR

As a check to determine if the anchor is dragging, attach a sounding lead or other heavy weight to a light line and put it over near the bow.

When the weight is on the bottom, tie off the line, leaving plenty of slack to account for possible swing of the vessel and the rise of the tide.

If the line goes taut, you know the anchor is dragging.

THE 28-FOOT LUGGER *PROCYON*, ENGLISH CHANNEL, AUGUST 19, 1878

Morning fine and sunny. Had the hose from the quay, and filled up water. 1 p.m., in a light W.S.W. breeze and a drizzly rain, I sailed out to the moorings and took them in. After luncheon, weighed both anchors and shifted my berth into deeper water. Intending to leave Dover in the morning, I stowed the kedge anchor away, and rode to the bower only, with 14 fathoms of chain fast to the cable buffer. Where bound to, it was impossible to say; as the weather was so thoroughly out of gear that the chances were many against any plan resolved upon overnight being practicable in the morning. The barometer was steady at 29.9, and yet the fitful drizzle of midday, that looked as if at any moment it might yield to the sun's power, changed into a continuous rain and thick haze as the afternoon advanced.

—R.T. McMullen

IF THE ANCHOR IS DRAGGING

Increase the scope—i.e., the amount of anchor line let out.

Set a second anchor.

Unmoor and then reset.

*A*ll hands unmoor! proclaims a boisterous cry;
All hands unmoor! the cavern'd rocks reply:
Roused from repose aloft the sailors swarm,
And with their levers soon the windlass arm:
The order given, up springing with a bound,
They fix the bars, and heave the windlass round;
At every turn the clanging pauls resound;
Up-torn reluctant from its oozy cave
The ponderous anchor rises o'er the wave.
High on the slippery masts the yards ascend,
And far abroad the canvas wings extend.

—William Falconer

Stackless anchor

The bottom of the sea is strewn with anchors.
—Henry David Thoreau

AUGUST

Monday
18
1998—Karen Thorndike arrived in San Diego, California, aboard the 36-foot cutter *Amelia*, the first woman to circumnavigate the globe singlehandedly by rounding the five great capes (Good Hope; Leeuwin, Australia; South East, Tasmania; Southwest, New Zealand; Horn).

Tuesday
19
1927—The cutter *Tally Ho* won the third Fastnet Race, from the Isle of Wight, England, to Fastnet Rock, Ireland, finishing in Plymouth, England; due to bad weather, only two of the fifteen starters finished.

Wednesday
20
1768—Captain James Cook, then a lieutenant, set sail in the ship *Endeavour* from Plymouth, England, on the first of his several voyages of exploration.

Thursday
21
1924—The Herreshoff Manufacturing Company of Bristol, Rhode Island, builders of yachts, naval vessels, and *America*'s Cup defenders, became a casualty of slow times after World War I and was sold off in lots to the highest bidders.

Friday
22
1994—The icebreaker *Louis S. St-Laurent* became the first Canadian surface ship to reach the North Pole.

Saturday
23
To its perfection, [the anchor's] size bears witness, for there is no other appliance so small for the great work it has to do.
—Joseph Conrad

Sunday
24
1927—The famed racing/fishing schooner *Columbia* was lost with all hands near Sable Island, Nova Scotia.

TO PROTECT YOUR BOAT FROM THEFT

Secure all openings.

Mount a motion-sensor floodlight on deck or in the rigging.

Set a motion-sensor sound and light alarm below decks.

Stow winch handles under lock and key, or otherwise hide them.

Rig a secret fuel shutoff valve and/or kill switch, and use them.

Install a time-delay shutoff valve and/or kill switch.

Secure the boat to a dock, piling, or permanent mooring with a chain and padlock.

Make the boat look occupied; most especially, float a dinghy astern.

THE CUTTER *SIRIUS*, MOORED AT VIGO, COAST OF SPAIN, AUGUST 29, 1921

R. did some very artistic painting to the yacht, and then we had a hard afternoon's shopping and some sight-seeing, after which dined and returned to the yacht at 10.00 p.m. To our dismay, when we got aboard we found the cabin door forced open. The yacht had been broken into by thieves. R. was the worst sufferer. His fine portmanteaux had been ruthlessly cut open, and valuables, camera, and clothes stolen thereout. This seemed about the last straw. I ought, of course, to have remembered that the code of morals in all big seaports is very different from those in the small ones, and had someone on board to guard the ship, but our long immunity from any contretemps of this sort had led to my forgetting it.
—C.F. Duncan

WITH TACKS SPRINKLED ON DECK, BUSINESS END UP

The port captain, a Chilean naval officer, advised me to ship hands to fight Indians in the strait [of Magellan] farther west…. I found only one man willing to embark, and he on condition that I should ship another "mon and a doog." But as no one else was willing to come along, and as I drew the line at dogs, I said no more about the matter, but simply loaded my guns. At this point in my dilemma Captain Pedro Samblich…gave me a bag of carpet-tacks, worth more than all the fighting men and dogs of Tierra del Fuego. I protested that I had no use for carpet-tacks on board. Samblich smiled at my want of experience, and maintained stoutly that I would have use for them. "You must use them with discretion," he said; "that is to say, don't step on them yourself." With this remote hint about the use of the tacks I got on all right, and saw the way to maintain clear decks at night without the care of watching.
—Joshua Slocum

TO PROTECT YOUR BOAT TRAILER FROM THEFT

Padlock the tongue hitch (the mechanism that holds the tongue to the ball).

Remove the tongue hitch from the trailer.

Secure the trailer to a fixed object with a heavy chain and padlock.

If the wheels have spokes or slots, chain them together.

Install a wheel lock device.

Set the trailer on blocks and remove at least one wheel.

By and large the fewer official holes there are in any boat the better unless adequately supervised.
—Peter Gerard

AUGUST

Monday
25
SUMMER BANK HOLIDAY / UK

1956—The Swedish warship *Vasa*, which rolled over and sank on her first sail in 1628, was located by divers virtually intact on the bottom of Stockholm Harbor.

Tuesday
26

1924—The *Wanderer*, the last square-rigged whaleship to sail out of New Bedford, Massachusetts, went aground off Cuttyhunk Island and was wrecked.

Wednesday
27

1893—More than 1,000 people drowned in Charleston alone when a hurricane struck the coast of South Carolina.

Thursday
28

1850—Messages were successfully sent via a submarine cable laid by the steamer *Goliath* from Dover, England, to Cape Grisnez, France; shortly thereafter, the cable broke, to be replaced a year later.

Friday
29

1878—The crew of the United States Coast Survey steamer *Drift* sighted what they took to be a sea serpent off Race Point, Cape Cod, Massachusetts.

Saturday
30

1925—The speedboat *Baby Bootlegger* won the 1925 Gold Cup on Manhasset Bay, Long Island, New York.

Sunday
31

1868—The first submarine telegraph cable from Britain to Denmark was completed.

A chart is a wonderfully fascinating thing.
—C. Fox Smith

THE SIZES OF CHARTS

Chart scales indicate the ratio of a given distance on the chart to the actual distance it represents on the Earth. A scale of 1:80,000 or 1/80,000 means that 1 unit (usually 1 inch) on the chart represents 80,000 units on the Earth.

A small-scale chart is one covering a relatively large area. A large-scale chart is one covering a relatively small area.

Sailing charts, for planning and offshore navigation, smaller than 1:600,000.

General charts, for coastwise navigation outside reefs and shoals, 1:150,000 to 1:600,000.

Coast charts, for inshore coastwise navigation, 1:50,000 to 1:150,000.

Harbor charts, for harbors and small waterways, larger than 1:50,000.

THE CHARM OF CHARTS, ACCORDING TO H.M. TOMLINSON

There is, we know, a pleasure more refined to be got from looking at a chart than from any impeccable modern map. Maps today are losing their attraction, for they permit of no escape, even to fancy. Maps do not allow us to forget that there are established and well-ordered governments up to the shores of the Arctic Ocean, waiting to restrict, to tax, and to punish us, and that their police patrol the tropical forests. But consider the legends of a chart even of the North Sea, of the world beneath the fathoms—the Silver Pits, the Dowsing Ground, the Leman Bank, the Great Fisher Ground, the Horn Reef, the Witch Ground, and the Great Dogger Bank.

THE MEANING OF CHARTS, ACCORDING TO ROCKWELL KENT

Charts have the same relation to the geography of the mariner's visual experience as four-dimensional geography has to the problems of everyday life: they picture in two dimensions what to the eye at sea appears in one.

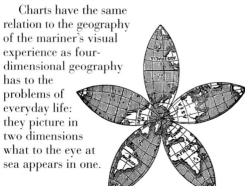

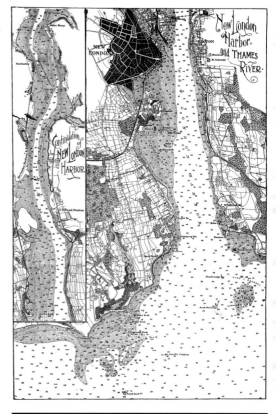

THE YACHT *TYPHOON*, OFF THE COAST OF FRANCE, SEPTEMBER 2, 1920

Cloudy. Wind N.W. Barograph high and steady. All slept late while *Typhoon* sailed herself under jib alone.

4 a.m. Fox went on deck and reported glow of two lights below horizon off port bow.

6:00 a.m. Lights proved to be two lighthouses, one on a small island.

7:00. W.W.N. prepares breakfast of oatmeal and tea as crew are still a bit groggy.

10:30. Raised mizzen and steered S.W. along French coast now plainly visible. The islands abeam seem to be Les Sept Isles as nearly as we can judge from our small scale chart.

11:30. Started motor to fetch point that makes out ahead of us.

1:30 p.m. Changed course to W. to clear outlying island which seems to be Tie de Batz. Slow work bucking strong head wind and tide and decide to put in instead of beating farther.

—William Washburn Nutting

*The nearer the land,
the greater the danger.*
—old saying

SEPTEMBER

Monday
1   LABOR DAY/ US & CANADA

1789—An Act of Congress required that a vessel's name and port of registry "be painted on her stern, on a black back ground with white letters of not less than three inches in length."

Tuesday
2

1935—A U.S. record low barometric pressure of 26.35 inches was set at Matecumbe Bay, Florida.

Wednesday
3

1878—The excursion steamer *Princess Alice*, with about 900 people aboard, primarily women and children, collided with the steamer *Bywell Castle* in the River Thames below Woolwich; only 200 survived.

Thursday
4

1963—John Trumpy, a founding director of the Mathis Yacht Building Company, and the owner of John Trumpy & Sons, builders of fine yachts, died in Annapolis, Maryland.

Friday
5

1966—The then-largest ship in the world, the 209,000-deadweight-ton tanker *Idemitsu Maru*, was launched near Tokyo, Japan.

Saturday
6

1937—The speedboat *Notre Dame* won the 1937 Gold Cup in Detroit, Michigan.

Sunday
7

1776—The American submarine *Turtle*, commanded by David Bushnell, was unsuccessful in an attempt to destroy HMS *Asia* in New York Harbor.

ANNALS OF STATE AND FEDERAL MERCHANT MARINE EDUCATION

1874—an Act of Congress authorized the U.S. Navy to lend ships to organizations educating young men in navigation and seamanship; the New York Nautical School, later the New York Maritime Academy, was the first to borrow a ship.

1891—a maritime academy was established in Pennsylvania.

1893—a maritime academy was established in Massachusetts.

1917—a six-week crash officer-training program was established by the United States Shipping Board for the World War I Emergency Fleet.

1929—a maritime academy was established in California.

1936—Congress passed the Merchant Marine Act, which authorized federal training for merchant marine officers.

1938—the U.S. Merchant Marine Cadet Corps, the nucleus of the U.S. Merchant Marine Academy, was established.

1941—a maritime academy was established in Texas.

1942—February; administration of the U.S. Merchant Marine Cadet Corps became the responsibility of the U.S. Coast Guard.

1942—July; administration of the U.S. Merchant Marine Cadet Corps became the responsibility of the War Shipping Administration.

1942—Congress appropriated funds to purchase the old Chrysler Estate at Kings Point, Long Island, New York, for a U.S. Merchant Marine Academy.

1942—Merchant Marine Cadet Schools were established in California and Mississippi.

1943—the U.S. Merchant Marine Academy, Kings Point, was dedicated.

TODAY'S AMERICAN MERCHANT MARINE ACADEMIES

California Maritime Academy, Vallejo, California

Great Lakes Maritime Academy, Traverse City, Michigan

Maine Maritime Academy, Castine, Maine

Maritime College, State University of New York, Throgs Neck, New York

Massachusetts Maritime Academy, Buzzards Bay, Massachusetts

Texas Maritime Academy, Galveston, Texas

U.S. Merchant Marine Academy, Kings Point, New York

THE SCHOONER-YACHT *MANDALAY*, OFF NEW YORK, SEPTEMBER 14, 1905

We passed safely out of the crowd of vessels, moving and at anchor, and got outside to find that we had all the canvas on her that she could carry comfortably. Good-sized rollers were coming in from the open sea, but the *Mandalay* rode them like a gull. As we passed the Sandy Hook Lightship, we took our departure and bore off to the Southwest, making nine knots, with great masses of gray foam rolling off to leeward from our forefoot and disappearing in the fog and darkness.

—Frank H. Trego

*T*he romance of the sea is a strange thing. It manages to cling to some extent to everything that floats, save and except possibly bucket dredgers and mud hoppers.

—C. Fox Smith

*To command is to serve,
nothing more and nothing less.*
    —André Malraux

SEPTEMBER

Monday
8

1827—A vessel carrying two bears, two foxes, a dog, fifteen geese, and several other animals, was sent over Niagara Falls, New York, as a publicity stunt; the vessel broke in half, one goose survived.

Tuesday
9

1721—Fredrik Henrik af Chapman, shipbuilder and naval architect, author of *Architectura Navalis Mercatoria*, vice admiral in the Swedish Navy, was born in Göteborg, Sweden.

Wednesday
10

1883—Joseph Conrad took a berth as second mate aboard the sailing ship *Riversdale* on a voyage from London, England, to Madras (now Chennai), India.

Thursday
11

1941—President Franklin Roosevelt ordered that any German or Italian naval vessels operating in U.S. territorial waters be attacked on sight.

Friday
12

1857—The American mail steamship *Central America* sank during a hurricane in the Atlantic Ocean off South Carolina with a consignment of three tons of gold on board; 400 lives were lost.

Saturday
13

1943—The U.S. Merchant Marine Academy, Kings Point, New York, was dedicated.

Sunday
14

1881—The Canadian sloop *Atalanta*, unsuccessful challenger for the *America*'s Cup, was launched in Belleville, Ontario.

SMALL-BOAT-SAILING DON'TS

Don't try to learn in anything but the best weather.

Don't be afraid to be afraid.

Don't be afraid to fear foul weather.

Don't be afraid to refuse to go sailing if you think the conditions are not favorable.

Don't take any passengers unless you have a lifesaving device for each.

Don't go sailing unless you know how to swim.

Don't get underway without the proper gear and safety equipment.

Don't skylark while underway.

Don't cleat the mainsheet.

Don't showboat in heavy weather; reduce sail as appropriate.

Don't try to ride the waves in the wake of a powerboat.

Don't get underway in the face of a storm, gale, or squall.

Don't sail in a fog without a compass.

Don't sail too close to obstructions, sandbars, buoys, ledges, etc.

Don't forget to keep an eye out for sudden gusts of wind, especially along shore.

Don't sail with water in the bilge; the free-surface effect can destabilize the boat.

Don't pinch pennies on maintenance, especially on your running rigging.

Don't sail at night without lights.

Don't assume that the other fellow knows the Rules of the Road.

Don't run downwind in a seaway if possible.

Don't sit on the lee side when sailing on the wind.

Don't lash the helm under any circumstances.

Don't overload the boat.

Don't sail in strange waters without a chart.

Don't try to tack into a large wave; wait for it to pass.

Don't jibe in heavy weather.

Don't panic if the boat capsizes.

Don't let go of the helm when underway.

Don't let sails or lines trail in the water.

Don't sail in a beam wind and sea if you can avoid it.

Don't "drink and drive."

Don't lose your head.

THE CUTTER *DRIAC II*, GULF OF FINLAND, SEPTEMBER 19, 1933

Nearly left *Driac* at the first anchorage we nosed into; daylight showed it to be just a little nest of rocks and reefs. Sailed into Hango 10.30 in morning, fresh N.E. wind, and tied up to the Yacht Club jetty in the smaller harbour. The town is a summer resort but was now practically shut up. Started blowing S.E. and we were banging up against the jetty, so got out and anchored in the middle of the harbour. In course of which we went over a shallow patch and knocked a few lumps out of it. No damage; in fact, never pumped the bilge out between Revel and Copenhagen.

—A.G.H. MacPherson

A small sailing craft is not only beautiful, it is seductive and full of strange promise and the hint of trouble. —E.B. White

SEPTEMBER

Monday
15

1789—James Fenimore Cooper, author of *The Pilot, the History of the Navy of the United States of America*, and *Leatherstocking Tales*, was born in Burlington, New Jersey.

Tuesday
16

1972—The 26-foot cruising yacht *Njord* was abandoned by her crew between France and the Balearic Islands (the crew was rescued); two weeks later, the yacht, sailing herself, was picked up by a Dutch freighter.

Wednesday
17

1852—Congress passed an act abolishing flogging as a punishment in the U.S. Navy.

Thursday
18

1984—Amyr Khan Klink of Brazil arrived in Praia di Espera, Brazil, at the end of the first solo row across the South Atlantic Ocean, from Bahia de Lüderitz, Namibia.

Friday
19

1957—The bathyscaph *Trieste* reached a record depth of two miles in the Mediterranean Sea.

Saturday
20

1892—The 3,539-ton four-masted bark *Roanoke*, then the largest wooden U.S. square-rigger in commercial service, was launched in Bath, Maine.

Sunday
21

1964—*Constellation* was successful in the nineteenth defense of the *America*'s Cup, defeating *Sovereign* of the Royal Thames Yacht Club.

IT TAKES THREE PEOPLE TO BUILD A BOAT

Two to do the work and one to take the blame when something goes wrong.

WE BUILD FOR THE AGES, SAYS JOHN RUSKIN

When we build, let us think that we build forever. Let it not be for present delight nor for present use alone. Let it be such work as our descendants will thank us for.

EXCELLENCE VS. PERFECTION

Careful workmanship, quality materials, and developing your skills is more important than a quest for perfection. Especially when building a first boat, excellence, not perfection, should be the goal.

—Henry "Mac" McCarthy

THE RISKS OF BOATBUILDING

Though banks lend people money to build boats now, such a practice was unheard of in my day. Boatbuilding and sailing were considered very high risk endeavors, and to my way of thinking, still are. You can lose all in a wink, insurance or no insurance.

—R.D. "Pete" Culler

THE BUSINESS OF BOATBUILDING

First year fighting all the way,
Second year spent in making hay,
Third and fourth and fifth he waxes,
Sixth year paying heavy taxes,
Seventh year come and he do fall,
No more boats to build at all.

—anon.

THE LIVE-OAK KELSONS, THE PINE PLANKS, THE SPARS, THE HACKMATACK-ROOTS FOR KNEES,

The ships themselves on their ways, the tiers of scaffolds, the workmen busy outside and inside,

The tools lying around, the great auger and little auger, the adze, bolt, line, square, gouge, and bead-plane.

—Walt Whitman

THE NAVAL DOCKYARD, PLYMOUTH, ENGLAND, SEPTEMBER 24, 1799

This morning Mr Whitford, coroner, took an inquest on a poor boy, who was carrying in to the dockyard his father's dinner while the bell at the gate was still ringing; the clapper fell off, struck the boy on the head, and fractured his skull in three places. Verdict, accidental death.

—from a contemporary report

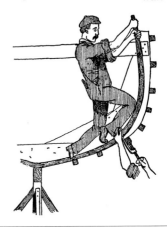

I have hunted wild boars and watched wild lions, built boats and killed many men.
—T.E. Lawrence

SEPTEMBER

Monday
22

1871—The celebrated tea clipper *Taeping*, second by a scant 28 minutes to the *Ariel* in the "Great Tea Race" of 1866 from China to England, was wrecked on a reef in the China Sea.

Tuesday
23   AUTUMNAL EQUINOX

1967—A storm that created waves as high as 25 feet struck a fleet of small boats fishing for coho salmon in northern Lake Michigan, capsizing many craft and driving nearly 200 ashore.

Wednesday
24

1995—Joseph Le Guen of France arrived in Molene, France, at the end of a solo row across the Atlantic Ocean from Chatham, Massachusetts.

Thursday
25

1909—The Hudson-Fulton Celebration, commemorating the tricentennial of the discovery of the Hudson River and the centennial of Robert Fulton's steamboat *Clermont*, got underway in New York.

Friday
26

1934—The RMS *Queen Mary* of the Cunard White Star Line, one of the last of the great transatlantic liners, was launched at Clydebank, Scotland.

Saturday
27   FIRST DAY OF ROSH HASHANAH

Sunday
28

The wonder is always new that any sane man can be a sailor.
—Ralph Waldo Emerson

THE BARK *SUNBEAM*, PACIFIC OCEAN, OCTOBER 4, 1864

Sunday. Reached the International Date Line, where all East bound vessels add a day to their week. On reaching the line, the captain said, "Today, we pass from East Longitude to West Longitude and we gain a day. That is, we have the same day twice, so tomorrow also will be Sunday." The stewardess nearly dropped the dish she was holding. The cook was openly defiant. When ordered to give the crew plum duff two days in succession, he grumbled about the sinfulness of serving a Sunday dinner on Monday, saying, "Give them plum duff again to-day! Never in all my going to sea did I cook plum duff on Monday! What's got the 'old man'? Two duff days together is contr'y to reason!"
—Alice Ranlett, wife of the captain

INTERNATIONAL DATE LINE

The International Date Line, the division between one day and the next, is not a straight line; rather, it is a zigzag modification of the 180th meridian. It was so drawn for political reasons and to include on one side of the line or another islands of groups that would otherwise have been divided. Vessels crossing the line on a westerly course lose a day: i.e., the date must be advanced one day. Vessels crossing it on an easterly course gain a day: i.e., the date must be set back one day.

KEEPING TRACK OF TIME

Time zone—a 15-degree interval between two meridians, one of 24 divisions of the Earth.
Greenwich Mean Time—the solar time at 0 degrees longitude, the Greenwich Meridian.
Zone time—the time in a given zone.

*T*he passage of time at sea
The watch is changed,
The glass is running.
We shall have a good voyage,
If God is willing.   —anon.

*T*hree bells!—"Keep a bright look-out there," sung out the lieutenant.
"Ay, ay, Sir," from the four look-out men, in a volley.
Then from the weather-gangway, "All's well," rose shrill into the night air.
—Michael Scott

A TIMEPIECE USED AS A COMPASS IN NORTHERN LATITUDES

Hold the timepiece horizontally, with the hour hand pointing directly toward the sun, or until the shadow of the hour hand falls directly beneath the hand itself. South will be halfway between the hour hand and 12 o'clock on the dial.

You may delay, but time will not.
—Benjamin Franklin

SEPT/OCT

Monday
29

1894—The 61-mile-long North Sea–Baltic Ship Canal—the Kiel Canal—was completed.

Tuesday
30

1997—With the success of GPS (Global Positioning System), the worldwide Omega electronic navigational system was discontinued.

Wednesday
1

1884—The International Meridian Conference was convened in Washington, D.C., to select as the Prime Meridian 0 degrees longitude, the meridian running through the Royal Observatory, Greenwich, England; France disagreed and continued to measure longitude from a point in Paris until 1911.

Thursday
2

1942—The Cunard White Star liner *Queen Mary*, serving as a wartime troop carrier, collided with and sank the light cruiser HMS *Curaçao* off the coast of Ireland.

Friday
3

1841—A northeast gale caught the Cape Cod fishing fleet at sea; at least 40 vessels were driven ashore; 57 men from the town of Truro alone lost their lives.

Saturday
4

Heavy weather is when the mode of handling the boat is dictated to you rather than by you.
—John Russell

Sunday
5

1864—A cyclone struck Calcutta, India; of approximately 200 major seagoing vessels driven ashore, most were unsalvageable.

SELF-RELIANCE

All the technology in the world will never change the fact that when your life is at stake, and the sea is your nemesis, the most useful equipment is that which helps you to help yourself.

—Charles J. Doane

DON'T LET GO

When Rudyard Kipling was a boy he went on a sea voyage with his father, Lockwood Kipling. Soon after the vessel got underway, Mr. Kipling went below, leaving Rudyard on deck. Presently there was a great commotion ahead, and one of the officers ran down and banged on Mr. Kipling's door.

"Mr. Kipling," he cried, "your boy has crawled out on the yardarm, and if he lets go, he'll drown."

"Yes," said Mr. Kipling, glad to know that nothing serious was wrong, "but he won't let go."

—from *The Sailor's Magazine and Seaman's Friend*, 1916

BE PREPARED, SAYS VANDERDECKEN

When a yacht is launched and all ready for sea, a yachtsman should resolutely go to work to make himself perfectly acquainted with the way in which things should be done; if he has had the advantage of owning a small craft previously matters will come very easy to him in a short time.

KEEP YOUR WEATHER EYE SHARP, SAYS CAPTAIN A.J. KENEALY

A man who ventures seaward in the morning in a balmy breeze and with the water smooth as a horsepond may be caught in a savage blow, followed by a heavy sea, in the afternoon.

A RULE TO LIVE BY, ACCORDING TO CARL LANE

A happy ship is a safe ship, and a safe ship is the only ship we want to sail. If I could not afford to make my boat safe, I'd stay ashore.

There is no dilemma compared with that of the deep-sea diver who hears the message from the ship above, "Come up at once. We are sinking."

—Robert Cooper

THE CLIPPER SHIP *SEA SERPENT*, INDIAN OCEAN, JUST WEST OF THE SUNDA STRAIT, OCTOBER 10, 1853

I was walking the quarter-deck with Mr. Cornell, the second mate, about a quarter past eleven o'clock, when the ship suddenly stopped, and shook so violently from stem to stern that every timber vibrated. This motion was accompanied by a dull rumbling, or rather humming noise, which seemed to come from under the stern. We were at first completely puzzled and bewildered by this unexpected circumstance, but a moment's reflection convinced us that it proceeded from an earthquake. Capt. Howland and Mr. Contee came on deck just in time to feel a second shock, nearly as violent as the first. Those who were below heard a strong hissing noise at the vessel's side. There did not appear to be any unusual agitation of the water, notwithstanding the vessel was so violently shaken.

—Bayard Taylor

A ship in a harbor is safe, but that's not what ships are built for.
—William Shedd

OCTOBER

Monday
6
YOM KIPPUR

1958—The nuclear submarine USS *Seawolf* set an underwater endurance record to date of 60 days.

Tuesday
7

1873—Washington J. Donaldson, attempting to cross the Atlantic Ocean from New York to Liverpool in a balloon fitted with a lifeboat, was brought down in Connecticut by a violent storm.

Wednesday
8

Gear which falls from aloft is usually harder than the head it falls upon. —John Irving

Thursday
9
LEIF ERICSSON DAY

1873—The United States Naval Institute, a professional society for those seeking to inject new thinking into the U.S. Navy, was established at Annapolis, Maryland.

Friday
10

1775—In the first written reference to the use of a vessel for pleasure in North America, Admiral Samuel Graves gave Dr. John Jeffries written permission to fish and shoot in Boston Harbor, Massachusetts.

Saturday
11

1846—The barometer fell 1.47 inches in six hours during a hurricane in Havana, Cuba.

Sunday
12

1861—The *Stag Hound*, the first very sharp or extreme clipper, caught fire and was destroyed off Pernambuco, Brazil; all hands were saved.

*Racin' every day of the week,
Every day except Sunday;
We finishes up of a Saturday night
And goes racin' again on Monday.*
—old sea song

CHOOSING HANDS FOR A RACING YACHT, LATE 19TH CENTURY, ACCORDING TO DIXON KEMP

Men widely differ in their smartness and in their habits; and a man may be tolerated in a racing yacht in spite of his moral delinquencies and faults of temper, because he is a very smart seaman, but a sloven should be given a very wide berth, as he will not only be offensive to the rest of the crew, but in all probability not a good seaman. As a rule, the smartest men (i.e., the cleverest and most active) are the most cleanly in their habits, the most prompt in doing their work, and in obeying orders, and the most satisfied, not to say proud, of their lot.... A sloven quarrels with the catering, with the work he has to do, with the liberty he gets, and with the places he visits. Such a man should find no berth in a racing yacht, and if a sailing master unfortunately ships such a creature, he should instantly unship.

THE 25 OLDEST AMERICAN YACHT CLUBS STILL IN EXISTENCE
New York Yacht Club, New York, 1844
Mobile Yacht Club, Alabama, 1847
Narragansett Yacht Club, Rhode Island, 1847
Pass Christian Yacht Club, Mississippi, 1849
Southern Yacht Club, Louisiana, 1849
Carolina Yacht Club, North Carolina, 1853
Buffalo Yacht Club, New York, 1860
Raritan Yacht Club, New Jersey, 1865
Riverton Yacht Club, New Jersey, 1865
Boston Yacht Club, Massachusetts, 1866
Detroit Yacht Club, Michigan, 1868
South Boston Yacht Club, Massachusetts, 1868
Portland Yacht Club, Maine, 1869
San Francisco Yacht Club, California, 1869
Savannah Yacht Club, Georgia, 1869
Eastern Yacht Club, Massachusetts, 1870
Lynn Yacht Club, Massachusetts, 1870
Milwaukee Yacht Club, Wisconsin, 1870
Beverly Yacht Club, Massachusetts, 1871
North Shore Yacht Club, New York, 1871
Seawanhaka Yacht Club, New York, 1871
Toms River Yacht Club, New Jersey, 1871
Santa Barbara Yacht Club, California, 1872
Albany Yacht Club, New York, 1873

A FOUL DAY FOR A RACE, OCTOBER 17, 1879

There started four sloops from Sandy Hook Lightship, for a race around the Cape May Lightship and return, for a cup valued at $700, offered some years previous by Mr. Robert Center, then the owner of the iron sloop *Vindex*. He had successfully kept her in commission for a whole winter, defying the gale with the stoutest of pilot boats, but creating an impression in the minds of the hardy toilers of the sea in those boats, as they saw the *Vindex* under short canvas bobbing like a cork on the ocean swell, that "the gentleman was not just right aloft." They were unable to realize that any sane man should go to sea in such weather for pastime.
—Captain R.F. Coffin

Yacht racing is an organized pastime, a function of social idleness ministering to the vanity of certain wealthy inhabitants.
—Joseph Conrad

OCTOBER

Monday
13
THANKSGIVING / CANADA
COLUMBUS DAY / US

1907—The legendary tea clipper *Thermopylae*, renamed *Pedro Nuñes* and converted to a coal barge by Portuguese owners, was towed to sea off the mouth of the Tagus River, Portugal, and sunk.

Tuesday
14

1889—John G. Hanna, author and designer of the Tahiti ketch, among other well-known cruising boats, was born.

Wednesday
15
DON'T FORGET TO ORDER THE 2004 EDITION OF THE MARINER'S BOOK OF DAYS

1854—At the conclusion of a race between the cutter-yachts *Viper* and *Belladonna* off Scituate, Massachusetts, the skipper of the *Viper* threw his foredeck man overboard for "slovenliness unbecoming a paid hand."

Thursday
16

1891—In an incident that came close to instigating war between the United States and Chile, American sailors ashore in Valparaiso, Chile, were attacked by a mob of civilians and police.

Friday
17

1941—Despite the lack of hostilities (at the time) between the United States and Germany, the destroyer USS *Kearny* was torpedoed by a German submarine off the coast of Iceland; the ship did not sink.

Saturday
18

1842—An underwater telegraphic cable, the first of its kind, was installed by Samuel F.B. Morse from Governor's Island in New York Harbor to Castle Garden.

Sunday
19

1848—The *John W. Cater*, the first ship to sail directly to San Francisco, California, in response to the discovery of gold, departed New York City.

DECOMMISSIONING A SMALL DAYSAILER FOR THE WINTER

Drain all water from the bilge.

Scrape all weed, shell, and marine growth from the bottom.

Scrub the topsides.

Block the keel firmly at several points.

Remove any inside ballast and clean it.

Remove running rigging and rinse in fresh water; coil and hang in a safe, dry place.

Remove all equipment and store in a safe, dry place.

Remove the sails, rinse in fresh water, spread to dry, then roll and store in a dry loft.

Remove spars, bundle with standing rigging, and store under cover in a way that provides support along their length.

WHEN LAYING UP A WOODEN BOAT

Pour automobile engine antifreeze into the bilge and allow it to remain there until spring. Besides preventing any water in the bilge from freezing, it is an excellent wood preservative and will kill algae and fungus that could lead to rot.

THE FIVE MOST IMPORTANT ELEMENTS OF BOAT STORAGE

Keep it clean.
Keep it dry.
Keep it ventilated.
Keep it secure.
Keep the boatyard happy (pay your bill on time).

THE 14-FOOT PAPER CANOE *MARIA THERESA*, HUDSON RIVER BELOW HUDSON CITY, NEW YORK, OCTOBER 22, 1874

At seven o'clock the river was mantled in a dense fog, but I pushed off and guided myself by the sounds of the running trains on the Hudson River Railroad…. Steamboats and tugs with canal-boats in tow were groping about the river in the misty darkness, blowing whistles every few minutes to let people know that the pilot was not sleeping at the wheel. There was a grand clearing up at noon; and as the sun broke through the mist, the beautiful shores came into view like a vivid flame of scarlet, yellow, brown, and green. It was the death-song of summer, and her dying notes the tinted leaves, each one giving to the wind a sad strain as it softly dropped to the earth, or was quickly hurled into space.

—Nathaniel H. Bishop

AN EXCELLENT TIME TO PAINT AND VARNISH IS IN THE FALL

Less dust and pollen in the air
Fewer bugs and insects around
Humidity is generally low
Less grinding and sanding by other boat owners in the boatyard than in the spring

Various ways to block the hull in a cradle

Until you do it all yourself you cannot have any idea of the innumerable minutiae to be attended to in the proper care of a yacht.
—John "Rob Roy" MacGregor

OCTOBER

Monday
20

1978—The U.S. Coast Guard Cutter *Cuyahoga*, after colliding with another vessel, sank in Chesapeake Bay near the mouth of the Potomac River; 11 coastguardsmen lost their lives.

Tuesday
21

1874—Nathaniel Holmes Bishop III began his voyage in the paper canoe *Maria Theresa* from Troy, New York, to Cedar Key, Florida. He wrote of his experiences in *The Voyage of the Paper Canoe*.

Wednesday
22

1934—Captain Alan Villiers and a crew of apprentices embarked in the square-rigged sailing ship *Joseph Conrad* from Harwich, England, on a voyage around the world.

Thursday
23

1903—HMS *Victory*, Nelson's flagship at the Battle of Trafalgar in 1805, was accidentally rammed by the battleship *Neptune*.

Friday
24

1817—The first advertisement for a proposed packet line providing regular transatlantic service between the United States and Europe appeared in the *Commercial Advertiser* of New York.

Saturday
25 DAYLIGHT SAVINGS ENDS / US & CANADA

Sunday
26 BRITISH SUMMER TIME ENDS / UK

A FEW MEASURES AND EQUIVALENTS TO ASSIST IN HISTORICAL READING

1 British cable = 608 feet =
 1/10 nautical mile
1 American cable = 720 feet
1 league = 3 statute miles =
 1/20 degree of latitude
1 statute mile = 5,280 feet =
 320 rods = 1,760 yards =
 1.6 kilometers
1 nautical mile = 6,076 feet =
 1,852 meters =
 1 minute of latitude
1 furlong = 1/8 statute mile =
 40 rods = 220 yards =
 201.7 meters
1 degree of latitude =
 362,753 feet = 20 leagues =
 60 nautical miles
1 fathom = 6 feet =
 1.82 meters
1 knot = 1 nautical mile per hour =
 1.15 statute miles per hour =
 101.27 feet per minute =
 1.8 kilometers per hour

KNOTS VERSUS KNOTS PER HOUR

Sticklers for accuracy never say "knots per hour," but such sticklers are rarely, if ever, nautical men. The seasoned seaman says "knots per hour" without a blush. And we can well now consider that "knot" is merely another term for "sea-mile."

—Geoffrey Prout,
Pocket-Book for Yachtsmen, 1930

CONVERSION TABLE

From	To	Multiply by
Inches	Centimeters	2.54
Centimeters	Inches	0.4
Feet	Centimeters	30.5
Centimeters	Feet	0.03
Yards	Meters	0.91
Meters	Yards	1.09
Square inches	Square centimeters	6.45
Square centimeters	Square inches	0.16
Square feet	Square meters	0.09
Square meters	Square feet	10.8
Square yards	Square meters	0.8
Square meters	Square yards	1.2
Pounds	Kilograms	0.45
Kilograms	Pounds	2.2
Ounces	Grams	28.4
Grams	Ounces	0.04

THE THREE-MASTED TOPSAIL-YARD SCHOONER, *SUNBEAM*, PACIFIC OCEAN, WEST OF VALPARAISO, CHILE, NOVEMBER 1, 1876

An almost calm day, with a few light showers, and fitful but unfavourable breezes. Some thirty or forty little birds, which the sailors called Mother Carey's chickens, but which were smaller and more graceful than any I have seen of that name, followed closely in our wake. I was never tired of watching the dainty way in which they just touched the tips of the waves with their feet, and then started off afresh, like a little maiden skipping and hopping along, from sheer exuberance of spirit.

—Lady Annie Brassey

It has always seemed to me that a bit of historical or romance reading about strange coasts adds much to the enjoyment of a cruise.
—Carl D. Lane

OCT/NOV

Monday
27

1899—The Gloucester schooner *Mary P. Mesquita*, fishing in a fog east of Cape Ann, was cut in two by the outward-bound Cunard liner *Saxonia*; the crew was rescued by the liner and taken to England.

Tuesday
28

1951—The tanker *Auris*, the first merchant ship powered by a gas turbine, got underway from Hebburn-on-Tyne, England, for Port Arthur, Texas, on her maiden voyage with her new power plant.

Wednesday
29

1837—The steamboat *Monmouth* collided with the ship *Trenton*, which was being towed by the steamboat *Warren*, near Prophet Island, Mississippi River; of 490 Creek Indians on the *Monmouth*, 234 perished.

Thursday
30

1808—Captain Benjamin Ireson of the schooner *Betty* was brought to justice in Marblehead, Massachusetts, for not going to the aid of a vessel in distress; he was tarred, feathered, and run out of town.

Friday
31 HALLOWEEN

1902—The first message was sent over the British Pacific undersea telegraphic cable between Canada and Australia, thus completing an all-British cable around the world.

Saturday ◐
1

1844—The Royal Bermuda Yacht Club, third oldest Royal Yacht Club in the world, was founded on the island of Bermuda.

Sunday
2

The sea was full of life and spirit.
—Sarah Orne Jewett

THE DOUBLE-PADDLE SAILING CANOE *AURORA*, OHIO RIVER, NOVEMBER 2, 1882

The wind came down with a howl as we approached Pomeroy, Ohio, opposite which is a long, low sandy point jutting into the stream, forcing the water through a narrow channel scarcely wider than a steamer's breadth. And as ill luck would have it, we here met an upward bound steamer. Unfortunately the *Aurora*'s lateen sails could not be taken from the mast nor lowered without coming up into the wind, and from the want of room I was unable to bear away. Thus I was forced to take my chances of being run down by the steamer or driven on to the bar by the force of the wind; but I escaped both and shot by clear.

—Dr. Charles A. Neide

THE CANOE DEFINED, ACCORDING TO DIXON KEMP, YACHT DESIGNER, LATE 19TH CENTURY

A canoe is a vessel propelled with a paddle or with sail by a person or persons facing forward; she is a vessel capable of navigating shallow water as well as open rough water; and she is a vessel not too large or too heavy for land portage by two men when her ballast and stores have been removed. Therefore, a vessel propelled by oars or machinery, which, either by bulk of hull or weight of fixed ballast cannot be lifted by two men, is not adapted to the requirements, nor entitled to the appellation.

THE FIRST SPRAY SKIRT WAS A MODIFIED COAT, FROM A LATE-19TH-CENTURY DESCRIPTION

For canoe travelling a macintosh coat is required. The coat is long, and closed in front from the bottom to the breast, where there is a neck opening with three buttons. Fixed by waterproof glue close under the arms is a macintosh flounce; run through the bottom hem of which is an elastic cord. The hem of the flounce is placed over the hatch and hatchway coaming, and abaft the backboard, thus forming a kind of tent. The object of having a long inside coat is that it will do duty as a macintosh for shore walking, the coat being then turned inside out, so that the flounce is out of sight.

I said to Lucine,"*Let's give up living in houses for a summer. We'll get a canoe, go off somewhere in Europe, and knock about the rivers.*"

"*Live for a summer in a canoe!*" *Lucine looked exclamation points at me.* "*Are you crazy?*"

—Melville Chater

*W*here the wave, as clear as dew,
Sleeps beneath the light canoe,
Which, reflected, floating there,
Looks as if hung in air
—T. Sturge Moore

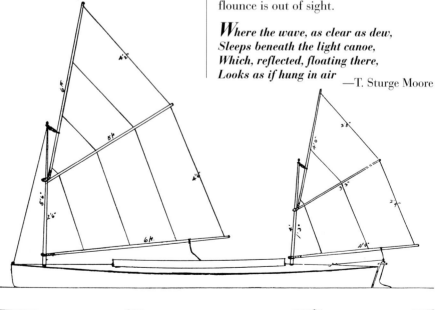

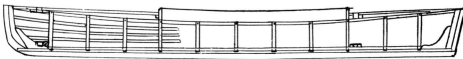

Sooner or later the spurious in a man's character will become apparent at sea.
—William McFee

NOVEMBER

Monday
3

1913—The fishing schooner *Annie M. Parker*, abandoned by her crew two days earlier after striking a shoal, was found sailing herself east of Nantucket by the British steamer *Astrakhan*.

Tuesday
4 ELECTION DAY

1766—Alexander Smith, also known as John Adams, one of the participants in the HMS *Bounty* mutiny and the last survivor of it, was born at Stanford Hill, Middlesex, England.

Wednesday
5 GUY FAWKES DAY / UK

1821—The *Savannah*, the first steam-powered vessel to cross the Atlantic, ran aground during a storm and broke up off Moriches, Long Island, New York.

Thursday
6

1869—Rear Admiral Charles Stewart, U.S. naval hero of the War of 1812 and commander of the frigate *Constitution* during her victory over HMS *Levant*, died in Bordentown, New Jersey.

Friday
7

1520—Ferdinand Magellan's fleet entered the Strait of the Eleven Thousand Virgins, now known as the Strait of Magellan, on the first passage of that strait from the Atlantic Ocean to the Pacific.

Saturday
8

1940—The *City of Bayville* struck a mine off Australia, thus becoming the first American merchant ship to be sunk during World War II.

Sunday ○
9

1913—Eight ore carriers sank with the loss of 270 lives on Lake Erie during a fierce gale that affected most of the Great Lakes region.

There is a vast difference between tying a knot and tying a good knot. While the one is an abomination, the other is a thing to admire.
—A. Hyatt Verrill

"*Haul out to leeward,*" comes at last,
  With a cheering from the fore and main;
"*Knot your reef-points, and knot them fast!*"
  Weather and lee are the ear-rings passed,
  And over the yard we bend and strain.

"*Lay down men, all; and now with a will,
  Swing on your topsail halyards, and sway;
Ease your braces and let her fill,
  There's an hour below of the mid-watch still,
  Haul taut your bowlines—well all—belay!*"
—from "Reefing Topsails," by Walter Mitchell

A SHANTYBOAT ON A BAYOU OFF THE MISSISSIPPI RIVER ABOVE NATCHEZ, NOVEMBER 16, 1949

We turned the boat around yesterday, so the main deck would be in the sun, and out of the N wind. Thinking of the hot days of summer and the power of the sun then, this move makes it a new season beyond a doubt. There is still much green in the woods, especially in the low river banks, but all is mellowing. The higher woods show wonderful color, not as bright as the northern maples, but new hues are seen, of dark dull tones, very exciting, the dark magnolias mingled with the brighter trees.
—Harlan Hubbard

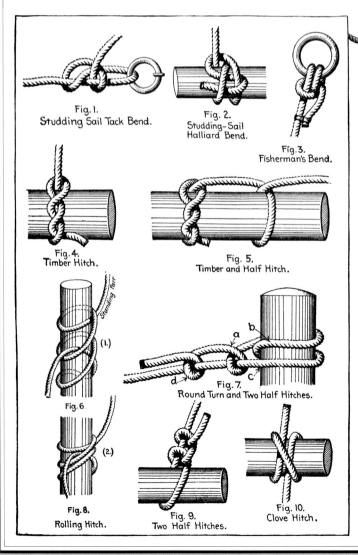

THE ELEMENTS OF A GOOD KNOT

Quickly and easily tied
Secure, without danger of slipping or loosening
Jam-free, yet easy to untie or cast off
Appropriate for its use

TECHNICALLY...

A knot is formed in the line itself: examples include the overhand, figure-of-eight, and reef knots, and the bowline.

A hitch is used to bend a line to another object, such as a bollard, a spar, or another line; examples include the clove, rolling, and half hitches.

A bend is used to join two lines together; examples include the sheet and carrick bends.

THE PARTS OF A KNOT

Standing part—the principal portion or longest part of the line

Bight—the portion that is bent or curved

End—the shorter portion of the line used in making the knot or splice

Long voyages, necessity, the reflection of mind engendered by calms, and endless experiments, evolve the perfect knots.
—Felix Riesenberg

NOVEMBER

Monday 10

1924—The raceboat *Farman Hydroglider*, driven by Jules Fisher, set a world propeller-driven water speed record of 87.392 mph, on the River Seine, France.

Tuesday 11

REMEMBRANCE SUNDAY / UK & CANADA
VETERANS DAY / US

1920—Lenah S. Higbee became the first woman to be awarded the U.S. Navy Cross, for her service during World War I.

Wednesday 12

DON'T FORGET TO ORDER THE 2004 EDITION OF THE MARINER'S BOOK OF DAYS

1942—The Liberty ship SS *Robert E. Peary*, built in the record time of 4 days, 15 hours, was launched.

Thursday 13

1850—Robert Louis Stevenson, author of *Kidnapped*, *Treasure Island*, and other novels with a maritime theme, was born in Edinburgh, Scotland.

Friday 14

1863—The full-rigged iron ship *Euterpe* was launched at the Isle of Man, Great Britain; renamed *Star of India* in 1906 and rerigged as a three-masted bark, she is currently a museum ship in San Diego, California.

Saturday 15

1853—The *Romance of the Seas*, the last extreme clipper ship built by Donald McKay for the California trade, was launched in East Boston, Massachusetts.

Sunday 16

1955—*Bluebird K7*, driven by Donald Campbell, set a world jet-powered water speed record of 216.2 mph on Lake Mead, Nevada.

A HEAD WIND

A contrary wind, I know not how, puts us all out of good humour; we grow sullen, silent and reserved, and fret at each other upon every little occasion.

—Benjamin Franklin

WIND STRENGTH IN THE LANGUAGE OF THE SAILOR

Living gale—a severe storm

Capful—a heavy wind

Black squall—a sudden strong wind that comes with a dark line on the surface of the sea

White squall—a sudden wind so strong that it turns the surface of the sea to white froth

Soldier's breeze—a fair, light wind

Ash breeze—a wind so light as to require oar power to move a sailing vessel

Gasoline breeze—same as above, for those who prefer motoring over rowing

Cat's paw—a small puff that ruffles the surface of the water

Irish hurricane—a flat calm

Paddy's hurricane—same as above

Blowing up and down—a dead calm

Flat-assed calm—same as above

If there is no wind, row.
   —old saying

THE SAILING SHIP *ELIZA*, OFF CAPE HORN, NOVEMBER 19, 1798

It would be an amusement to an indifferent spectator to observe the Woefull looks of our crew when we have one of our Dismal head Winds, and to see how soon they clear up when it changes, and we can well say that not only our feelings but likewise our looks depends on the Wind, so one may easily judge how often they vary…. I have got so inur'd to bad Weather and a head Wind that they have but a small effect on my ease, and were our Forecastle not so wet and disagreeable, I should enjoy myself as well here as I ever did on shore.

—William Sturgis

FROM "EVENING ON THE HARBOR"
by Dexter Carlton Washburn

As I drift in my boat on the harbor,
In the calm of the summer night,
The moon in the arms of the crescent
Floods all with its misty light.

The water reflects the moon-beams
In a wavy, twisted band,
Like a mirror of polished metal
From some distant Eastern land.

No sound but the click of the rowlock,
And the measured dip of an oar,
And the lisping plash of the ripples,
As they break on the western shore.

Stark calms are a wearisom business.
—Ralph Stock

NOVEMBER

Monday ◐
17

1791—The value of rations per man in the Revenue-Marine, forerunner of the U.S. Coast Guard, was set by the Treasury Department at 12 cents per day.

Tuesday
18

1798—A number of seamen were taken from the U.S. sloop-of-war *Baltimore* by a British press gang; later, the U.S. Navy directed its commanders to resist such impressments, by the force of arms if necessary.

Wednesday
19

1939—Felix Riesenberg, deepwater sailor and author of *Under Sail*, *Cape Horn*, and other books of the sea, died in New York City.

Thursday
20

1808—William Hackett, builder of many of the greatest American ships of the late 18th century, including the naval frigates *Alliance* and *Essex*, died in Salisbury, Massachusetts.

Friday
21

1915—The British ship *Endurance*, bound for an overland expedition in Antarctica, sank in the Weddell Sea after having been abandoned in the pack ice by Ernest Shackleton and his crew.

Saturday
22

1916—Jack London—hobo, socialist, war correspondent, author of *The Sea Wolf*—died near Santa Rosa, California.

Sunday
23

A great mind is a good sailor, as a great heart is.
—Ralph Waldo Emerson

HMS *LIZARD*, QUEBEC CITY, ST. LAWRENCE RIVER, NOVEMBER 24, 1775

AM the Carpenters from the Shore begun to Clap Bulge ways under the Off Side of the Ship to Keep her from Receiving any Damage. Empd Getting Our Bread and Other Stores out of the Schooner & Snow to Proper Store houses Alloted for them. Punished Geo Watson & Thos Killian with 1 Dozen Lashes each for Drunkeness & Neglect of Duty. The first Part Light Breezes and Cloudy middle & Latter fresh Breezes With Clear Wr & hard frost. PM Punished Martin Fling with 1 Dozen Lashes for Drunkeness & neglect of Duty & mutiny and put him in Confinement. Employ'd Clearing the Above mentioned Stores.
—Captain John Hamilton

A NIGHT AT DAGO TOM'S
by John Masefield

*Oh yesterday, I t'ink it was, while cruisin'
  down the street,
I met with Bill— "Hullo," he says, "let's give
  the girls a treat."
We'd red bandanas round our necks 'n' our
  shrouds new rattled down,
So we filled a couple of Santy Cruz and
  cleared for Sailor Town.*

*We scooted south with a press of sail till we
  fetched to a caboose,
The "Sailor's Rest," by Dago Tom, alongside
  "Paddy's Goose."
Red curtains to the windies, ay, 'n' white sand
  to the floor,
And an old blind fiddler liltin' the tune of
  "Lowlands No More."*

*He played the "Shaking of the Sheets" 'n' the
  couples did advance,
Bowing, stamping, curtsying, in the shuffling
  of the dance;
The old floor rocked and quivered, so it struck
  beholders dumb,
'N' arterwards there was sweet songs 'n' good
  Jamaikey rum.*

*'N' there was many a merry yarn of many a
  merry spree
Aboard the ships with royals set a-sailing on
  the sea,
Yarns of the hooker "Spindrift," her as had the
  clipper-bow,—
"There ain't no ships," says Bill to me, "like
  that there hooker now."*

*When the old blind fiddler played the tune of
  "Pipe the Watch Below,"
The skew-eyed landlord dowsed the glim and
  bade us "Stamp 'n' go,"
'N' we linked it home, did Bill 'n' I, adown the
  scattered streets,
Until we fetched to Land o' Nod atween the
  linen sheets.*

**SERIOUS LIQUID MEASURES
(IN IMPERIAL GALLONS)**

Pipe of Port, 115
Pipe of Teneriffe, 100
Pipe of Marsala, 93
Pipe of Madeira and Cape, 92
Pipe of Lisbon and Bucellas, 117
Butt of Sherry and Tent, 108
Aum of Hock and Rhenish, 30
Hogshead of Claret, 46
Hogshead of Port, 57
Hogshead of Sherry, 54
Hogshead of Madeira, 46
Hogshead of Ale, 54
Butt of Ale, 108

I think the modern desire to go to sea for fun must be all to the common good. The world has to be explored anew.
—H.M. Tomlinson

NOVEMBER

Monday 24

1942—The SPARS, the women's branch of the U.S. Coast Guard, was established. The acronym is derived from *Semper Paratus* (Always Ready), the Coast Guard motto.

Tuesday 25

1837—Captain Thomas H. Sumner, at sea between Ireland and Wales on a voyage between South Carolina and Scotland, took a sun sight through the clouds and from it developed a technique of navigation since known as Sumner's Line.

Wednesday 26

1890—The magnificent wooden four-masted bark *Shenandoah*, so beautiful that her image would appear on the sailing licenses of all American masters, was launched in Bath, Maine.

Thursday 27 THANKSGIVING

1926—The knockabout *Helen B. Thomas*, the first Gloucester fishing schooner rigged without a bowsprit, was destroyed by fire while serving as a Bermuda pilot boat.

Friday 28

1773—The *Dartmouth*, first of the East India tea ships that would become central to the celebrated Boston Tea Party, arrived in Boston Harbor, Massachusetts.

Saturday 29

1791—The king of France granted John Fitch, an American, a patent for a steam-propelled vessel.

Sunday 30   ADVENT SUNDAY / ST. ANDREW'S DAY / UK

GLOSSARY OF SELECTED SHIPPING TERMS

Act of God—an event that occurs without the intervention of man, such as a flood, gale, earthquake, etc.

Arrest—detention of a vessel.

Bareboat charter—charterer hires its own crew and pays the operating expenses.

Barratry—an illegal or fraudulent act by the officers or crew to the detriment of the owner.

Bill of health—a document indicating the condition of the health of the country from which the vessel sailed.

Bill of lading—a receipt for cargo on board; evidence of title to the cargo.

Bonded goods—imported goods stored in a government warehouse until duty is paid on them.

Consignee—the person or company authorized to receive the cargo.

Constructive total loss—the cost of salvaging and repairing a wrecked vessel exceeds her value as a whole.

Demurrage—money paid as damage for delay in shipment.

Derelict—a vessel that has been abandoned but has not sunk.

Flotsam—cargo lost or thrown overboard that remains afloat.

Free on board—cargo delivered on board a ship without shipping charges to the purchaser.

Indemnity—security from damage or loss.

Jetsam—cargo lost or thrown overboard that sinks; also such cargo that later washes ashore.

Jettison—to throw cargo overboard to save the vessel.

Lagan—cargo thrown overboard with a buoy attached so it can be recovered later.

Lay days—days spent in port loading or discharging cargo.

Lighterage—a charge payable for loading or unloading a ship by lighter or barge.

Load line—a mark on the side of a ship indicating the depth in the water to which a ship may be loaded.

Manifest—a list of passengers, stores, and cargo on board.

Pratique—permission to land the crew, passengers, and cargo after all health regulations have been satisfied.

Quayage—a charge for berthing alongside a quay, wharf, or pier; aka wharfage.

Salvage—money paid to those who have salvaged, or assisted in the salvage of, a vessel.

Ship's articles—employment agreement between the master and the crew.

Ship's husband—the agent who superintends a vessel when in port.

Supercargo—abbreviation for "cargo superintendent"; representative of the owner who looks after the cargo.

Time charter—the charterer has the use of a vessel for a specified period of time.

Voyage charter—the charterer has the use of a vessel for a single voyage.

Wharfage—see Quayage, above.

THE SHIPBUILDING TOWN OF THOMASTON, MAINE, DECEMBER 4, 1850

Morton had trouble to-day in launching his vessel: It seems that one side of the ways was fifteen feet longer than the other and that caused her to go over on her side, her masts in the water and her keel out, and there she now lies with her decks up and down.

The ship *Telamon*, Capt. Snow, sailed to-day and is having a fine chance off.

—Captain Charles E. Ranlett

Sailors are simple, light-hearted souls, whose load of yesterday is airy as thistle-down today.
—Arthur Mason

DECEMBER

Monday
1

1842—Midshipman Philip Spencer (son of the Secretary of the Navy), Boatswain Samuel Cromwell, and Seaman Elisha Small of the USS *Somers* were executed for mutiny.

Tuesday
2

1999—A shipping container containing Nike cross-trainers went overboard in the Pacific Ocean from the P&O containership *Nedlloyd Auckland*; a year later, the shoes began appearing on the beaches of the Pacific Northwest.

Wednesday
3

I had all the wonder of that great still sea, I had all the beauty of that spreading sky, I had all the magic of complete tranquility. —Vere Hutchinson

Thursday
4

1868—The steamboats *United States* and *America* collided on the Ohio River near Warsaw and burned with great loss of life.

Friday
5

In a ship you are constantly reminded of how much you depend on your fellow sailors. —Douglas Reeman

Saturday
6

1988—The Swedish warship *Vasa*, sunk in 1628 and raised intact in 1961, was moved to a new museum built specially for her in Stockholm, Sweden.

Sunday
7

1881—The *Meefoo*, the first steamer sailing under the Chinese flag to trade with Britain, arrived in the River Thames with 3,000 tons of tea for London.

HOW MUCH SAIL AREA IS ENOUGH?

Too little can be frustrating.
Too much can be overwhelming.
The ideal is the amount the boat can stand up to and the crew can reasonably handle in all conditions.

SAIL AREA RULES OF THUMB, CRUISING BOATS

Sail area in square feet = square of the waterline length
—or—
100 square feet of sail for every ton of displacement.

IN THE SELECTION OF CANVAS FOR MAKING A SUIT OF SAILS, A YACHTSMAN CANNOT BE TOO PARTICULAR, SAYS VANDERDECKEN

Whether good or bad material be put in them, the cost of making will all be the same; but badly woven canvas will not last in form or work any length of time, whereas a first-rate material when well cut and made up, if it receives fairplay in the handling, will work until the last rag leaves the bolt ropes; therefore the worst economy a yachtsman can exercise is in clipping down and paring the expenditure under the head of sails.

THE COMPONENTS OF CANVAS

Warp—the threads running lengthwise
Weft—the threads running crosswise
Selvage—the finished edge

THE MAJOR PARTS OF A SAIL

Cloths—the panels of fabric
Seams—the sewn joints of the cloths

OLD-STYLE PRESERVATIVE FOR WORKBOAT SAILS

1 gallon cod-liver oil
3 pails salt water
Red ochre for the color and consistency desired
Apply it with a broom.
Spread sails out horizontally to dry.

MORE REFINED OLD-STYLE PRESERVATIVE FOR PLEASURE-BOAT SAILS

Boil a few pounds of cutch and a few lumps of mutton fat in a kettle of fresh water.
Immerse the sail in the hot liquid; remove sail after liquid has cooled, and hang up to dry.

THE YAWL *AMARYLLIS*, CARIBBEAN SEA, DECEMBER 12, 1920

The second day out was overcast and rainy, but I managed to get a sight for a position line at 8 a.m., and also the meridian altitude, which I was glad to be able to do, as the currents into the Caribbean are very uncertain, and depend largely on the strength of the Trade Wind, and on the Equatorial Current. Soon after noon we sighted Tobago on the right bearing. At dusk the north end of the island was abeam, distant 15 miles. I kept well to the eastward of the Bocas de Dragos, as the current between Grenada and Trinidad sometimes runs at 3 knots to the westward.
—G.H.P. Muhlhauser

There is no pastime that yields such a splendid return for one's money as that of cruising in small yachts.
—Francis B. Cooke

DECEMBER

Monday
8

1891—Bath Iron Works of Bath, Maine, one of the oldest commercial shipyards currently operating in the United States, launched its first vessel, the gunboat *Machias* for the U.S. Navy.

Tuesday
9

1901—Pat McGiehan, of Jersey City, New Jersey, best-known builder of fast racing sandbaggers, died.

Wednesday
10

1905—Relief Lightship 50, on station at the Nantucket Shoals, sank in a gale; the crew was rescued by the lighthouse tender *Azalea*.

Thursday
11

1954—The first aircraft carrier with an angled flight deck, the USS *Forrestal*, was launched in Newport News, Virginia.

Friday
12

There, sailing the sea, we play every part of life: control, direction, effort, fate; and there we can test ourselves and know our state.   —Hilaire Belloc

Saturday
13

1693—Willem van de Velde the Elder, Dutch marine painter, died in Amsterdam.

Sunday
14

1945—Captain Sue Sophia Dauser, U.S. Navy, became the first nurse to be awarded the Distinguished Service Medal.

CHANNEL PASSAGE
by Rupert Brooke

*The damned ship lurched and slithered. Quiet
  and quick
My cold gorge rose; the long sea rolled; I knew
I must think hard of something, or be sick;
And could think hard of only one thing—you!
You, you alone could hold my fancy ever!
And with you memories come, sharp pain, and
  dole.
Now there's a choice—heartache or tortured
  liver!
A sea-sick body, or a you-sick soul.*

*Do I forget you? Retchings hoist and tie me,
Old meat, good meals, brown gobbets, up I
  throw.
Do I remember? Acrid return and slimy,
The slobs and slobber of a last year's woe.
And still the sick ship rolls. 'Tis hard, I tell ye,
To choose 'twixt love and nausea, heart and
  belly.*

THE QUAHOG SKIFF *BUGSY'S BOOMER*, BILLINGSGATE SHOAL, CAPE COD BAY, DECEMBER 19, 1956

So it came on to lunch. Fred was eating an oily-looking sausage bomb and going on and on about how the shellfish warden was a dime-store nutcase and if brains were dynamite he wouldn't have enough to blow his nose and "Hell's hairy bells, that guy's so stupid he.... hey! anyone got a drink?" Larry dug around under the floorboards and came up with a can of beer. Fred said thanks, popped the top, took a pull, belched, bit off another piece of the bomb, took another pull, and went back to deconstructing the warden. And that's when we were hit by a set of the nastiest cresting waves you're ever going to see. The skiff nearly rolled over. Fred turned sort of grayish-green. Suddenly he said, "I feel funny," stumbled to the rail, and—how should we say?—proceeded to chum for the whales.

—E.H. Morgan

TO PREVENT SEASICKNESS

Before getting underway and while at sea: avoid heavy meals, particularly fried food, and alcohol.

Remain on deck in the fresh air.

Keep your eyes on the horizon.

Position yourself amidships, where motion is least.

Anticipate the vessel's motion.

Keep warm on cold days and cool on hot days.

Don't smoke; get upwind from those who do.

FOUR SUREFIRE WAYS TO BRING ON SEASICKNESS WHEN UNDERWAY IN FOUL WEATHER

Read a book, especially one with fine print.

Remain below decks.

Use binoculars for extended periods.

Have a sausage bomb for lunch...

...with a beer chaser.
—Fred Brooks

Were it not for sea-sickness, the whole world would be sailors.
—**Charles Darwin**

DECEMBER

Monday 15

1909—The six-masted schooner *Wyoming*, largest wooden schooner ever built—329 feet length, 50 feet beam, 30 feet draft—was launched in Bath, Maine.

Tuesday 16

1773—Colonials dressed as Indians dumped tea from the British ships *Dartmouth*, *Eleanor*, and *Beaver* in a rebellious act that would become known as the Boston Tea Party.

Wednesday 17

1939—The German pocket battleship *Admiral Graf Spee* was scuttled off Montevideo, Uruguay, after an action with three British cruisers.

Thursday 18

1944—The U.S. Navy's Task Force 38, en route to Luzon, Philippines, was struck by a fierce typhoon in the Pacific Ocean. Three destroyers capsized and were lost; several other ships were severely damaged.

Friday 19

1861—The clipper ship *Empress of the Seas* burned in Queenscliffe, Australia.

Saturday 20   FIRST DAY HANUKKAH

1822—The U.S. Congress authorized a 14-ship squadron to suppress piracy in the Caribbean.

Sunday 21

1850—The extreme clipper ship *Witchcraft* was launched in Chelsea, Massachusetts.

SAILING SHIPS ARE ENCHANTING, ACCORDING TO JOHN RUSKIN

There is not, except the very loveliest creatures of the living world, anything in nature so absolutely notable, bewitching, and, according to its means and measure, heart-occupying, as a well-handled ship under sail in a stormy day.

NASTY BUT LOVABLE, SAYS REX CLEMENS

The sailing ship was an exacting mistress to serve. She was all that; she was a heart-breaking wench at times, yet none the less a Cleopatra among the sisterhood of the sea, inspiring an affection the lady-like liner is powerless to evoke.

AND LIVING BEINGS, SAYS CAPTAIN ARTHUR H. CLARK

A sailing ship is an exceedingly complex, sensitive, and capricious creation—quite as much so as most human beings. Her coquetry and exasperating deviltry have been the delight and despair of seamen's hearts, at least since the days when the wise, though much-married, Solomon declared that among the things that were too wonderful for him and which he knew not, was "the way of a ship in the midst of the sea."

*T*here be three things which are too wonderful for me, yea, four which I know not:
    The way of an eagle in the air; the way of a serpent upon a rock; the way of a ship in the midst of the sea; and the way of a man with a maid.

—Proverbs 30

THE SAILING VESSEL *SANTA CLARA*, ATLANTIC OCEAN, SOUTHEAST OF NEW YORK, DECEMBER 25, LATE 19TH CENTURY

At long last, the topsail was reefed, the ship shortened down and we were told to go below and get our dinner.... I had been hungry until I got back into my room. The door had been left on the hook, open a crack only. The old *Santa Clara*, a notoriously wet brute, had shipped a heavy sea over the weather rail and everything in my room was afloat. After I had succeeded in bailing and swabbing out my room, I plumped down on the donkey for my dinner. The coffee was cold, the beef was greasy and the bread soggy. I saw in my mind's eye my brother and sister sitting at table surrounded by turkey, "stuffing and fixings," mince, pumpkin, apple and custard pies, and all the other good things in keeping with a Down East Christmas dinner. My appetite was gone. For the only time in my life I was homesick. My bedclothes and mattress were wet and I was very unhappy.

—Eugene Henry, ship's boy

It is impossible not to personify a ship.
—Ralph Waldo Emerson

DECEMBER

Monday
22 WINTER SOLSTICE

1837—The U.S. Congress passed the first bill authorizing public vessels—specifically, cutters of the Revenue-Marine, forerunner of the U.S. Coast Guard—to go to the aid of distressed mariners.

Tuesday
23

The Ship seemed alive whilst she floated with proud fearlessness into the mystery of the night.   —W. Clark Russell

Wednesday
24

1814—The signing of the Treaty of Ghent ended the War of 1812, during which most American naval traditions were established.

Thursday
25 CHRISTMAS DAY

1717—The coast of Friesland, on the North Sea, was inundated by a great gale-driven flood; more than 2,700 people and 16,000 cattle were drowned, and more than 1,000 houses were destroyed.

Friday
26 FIRST DAY OF KWANZAA
BOXING DAY / UK & CANADA
ST. STEPHEN'S DAY HOLIDAY / UK

1873—A gale swept the northeast U.S. coast, sinking and damaging several ships, including the *Peruvian*, which went ashore on the Peaked Hill Bar, Cape Cod, with the loss of all hands, and three miles south of her, the German bark *Francis*, whose crew was saved.

Saturday
27

1925—The *Edward J. Lawrence*, the last six-masted schooner afloat, was burned in Portland, Maine.

Sunday
28

Ships are what men make them.
—Joseph Conrad

THE JOY OF LANDFALL, I

After dinner one of our mess went up aloft to look out, and presently announced the long-wished for sound, Land! Land! In less than an hour we could descry it from the deck, appearing like tufts of trees. I could not discern it so soon as the rest; my eyes were dimmed with the suffusion of two small drops of joy.
—Benjamin Franklin

THE JOY OF LANDFALL, II

It was the *Snark*'s first landfall—and such a landfall! For twenty-seven days we had been on the deserted deep, and it was pretty hard to realize that there was so much life in the world. We were made dizzy by it. We could not take it all in at once.
—Jack London

*T*he best noise in all the world is the rattle of the anchor chain when one comes into harbor at last and lets it go over the bows.
—Hilaire Belloc

THE CLIPPER SHIP *SEA SERPENT*, SOUTH ATLANTIC OCEAN, NORTHWEST OF CAPE TOWN, DECEMBER 30, 1854

At 5 A.M. a sail was discovered ahead, a point off starboard bow. At 7 A.M., wind dead aft, squared yards and set studding sails, both sides, and then began to overhaul the sail fast. At 10 A.M. made her out to be a full-rigged ship under a cloud of canvas (main skysail, royal studding sails, etc.).... At 3 she was within hailing distance and proved to be the *Ariel*, Captain Ayres, which sailed ten days before us.... It was the noblest sight I ever saw, to see the *Ariel*, one mass of canvas (having thirty-two sails set), rising and sinking in the swell like a thing of life. A bright moonlight night. At midnight the *Ariel* could be seen, when the moon shone fair on her sails, about a mile astern. Hauled down lee main studding sails.
—Hugh McCulloch Gregory

FINALLY HOME

When at last the passage perilous has been won, and the little yacht lies at rest in some delectable haven, the past discomfort is forgotten and one thinks only of the successful issue of the struggle with the elements.
—Francis B. Cooke

*T*he stately ship is seen no more,
The fragile skiff attains the shore;
And while the great and wise decay,
And all their trophies pass away,
Some sudden thought, some careless rhyme,
Still floats above the wrecks of Time.
—William Edward Hartpole Lecky

*Oh, was there ever sailor free to choose,
That didn't settle somewhere near the sea?*
—Rudyard Kipling

DEC/JAN

Monday
29

1955—Dr. Hannes Lindemann, who was studying the effects of hardship at sea, landed at St. Croix, Virgin Islands, following a voyage from Las Palmas, Canary Islands, in a sailing dugout log canoe.

Tuesday
30

1935—The Historic American Merchant Marine Survey, a New Deal program to document the shape and breadth of traditional maritime America, was established.

Wednesday
31 NEW YEAR'S EVE

1948—Sir Malcolm Campbell, holder of several records for speed on the water, died in Reigate, Surrey, England.

Thursday
1 NEW YEAR'S DAY

1959—The U.S. Naval Observatory in Washington, D.C., began keeping "atomic time," using cesium beam atomic oscillators.

Friday
2

1991—Irving Johnson, sailor, adventurer, and author of *Peking Battles Cape Horn* and other books, died in Hadley, Massachusetts.

Saturday
3

1907—Johann Klepper of Rosenheim, Germany, a tailor by trade, introduced the first successful folding kayak.

Sunday
4

The land holds more perils
for the seaman than the sea.
—anon.

2003

January
S	M	T	W	T	F	S
			1	2	3	4
5	6	7	8	9	10	11
12	13	14	15	16	17	18
19	20	21	22	23	24	25
26	27	28	29	30	31	

February
S	M	T	W	T	F	S
						1
2	3	4	5	6	7	8
9	10	11	12	13	14	15
16	17	18	19	20	21	22
23	24	25	26	27	28	

March
S	M	T	W	T	F	S
						1
2	3	4	5	6	7	8
9	10	11	12	13	14	15
16	17	18	19	20	21	22
23	24	25	26	27	28	29
30	31					

April
S	M	T	W	T	F	S
		1	2	3	4	5
6	7	8	9	10	11	12
13	14	15	16	17	18	19
20	21	22	23	24	25	26
27	28	29	30			

May
S	M	T	W	T	F	S
				1	2	3
4	5	6	7	8	9	10
11	12	13	14	15	16	17
18	19	20	21	22	23	24
25	26	27	28	29	30	31

June
S	M	T	W	T	F	S
1	2	3	4	5	6	7
8	9	10	11	12	13	14
15	16	17	18	19	20	21
22	23	24	25	26	27	28
29	30					

July
S	M	T	W	T	F	S
		1	2	3	4	5
6	7	8	9	10	11	12
13	14	15	16	17	18	19
20	21	22	23	24	25	26
27	28	29	30	31		

August
S	M	T	W	T	F	S
					1	2
3	4	5	6	7	8	9
10	11	12	13	14	15	16
17	18	19	20	21	22	23
24	25	26	27	28	29	30
31						

September
S	M	T	W	T	F	S
	1	2	3	4	5	6
7	8	9	10	11	12	13
14	15	16	17	18	19	20
21	22	23	24	25	26	27
28	29	30				

October
S	M	T	W	T	F	S
			1	2	3	4
5	6	7	8	9	10	11
12	13	14	15	16	17	18
19	20	21	22	23	24	25
26	27	28	29	30	31	

November
S	M	T	W	T	F	S
						1
2	3	4	5	6	7	8
9	10	11	12	13	14	15
16	17	18	19	20	21	22
23	24	25	26	27	28	29
30						

December
S	M	T	W	T	F	S
	1	2	3	4	5	6
7	8	9	10	11	12	13
14	15	16	17	18	19	20
21	22	23	24	25	26	27
28	29	30	31			

2002

January
S	M	T	W	T	F	S
		1	2	3	4	5
6	7	8	9	10	11	12
13	14	15	16	17	18	19
20	21	22	23	24	25	26
27	28	29	30	31		

February
S	M	T	W	T	F	S
					1	2
3	4	5	6	7	8	9
10	11	12	13	14	15	16
17	18	19	20	21	22	23
24	25	26	27	28		

March
S	M	T	W	T	F	S
					1	2
3	4	5	6	7	8	9
10	11	12	13	14	15	16
17	18	19	20	21	22	23
24	25	26	27	28	29	30
31						

April
S	M	T	W	T	F	S
	1	2	3	4	5	6
7	8	9	10	11	12	13
14	15	16	17	18	19	20
21	22	23	24	25	26	27
28	29	30				

May
S	M	T	W	T	F	S
			1	2	3	4
5	6	7	8	9	10	11
12	13	14	15	16	17	18
19	20	21	22	23	24	25
26	27	28	29	30	31	

June
S	M	T	W	T	F	S
						1
2	3	4	5	6	7	8
9	10	11	12	13	14	15
16	17	18	19	20	21	22
23	24	25	26	27	28	29
30						

July
S	M	T	W	T	F	S
	1	2	3	4	5	6
7	8	9	10	11	12	13
14	15	16	17	18	19	20
21	22	23	24	25	26	27
28	29	30	31			

August
S	M	T	W	T	F	S
				1	2	3
4	5	6	7	8	9	10
11	12	13	14	15	16	17
18	19	20	21	22	23	24
25	26	27	28	29	30	31

September
S	M	T	W	T	F	S
1	2	3	4	5	6	7
8	9	10	11	12	13	14
15	16	17	18	19	20	21
22	23	24	25	26	27	28
29	30					

October
S	M	T	W	T	F	S
		1	2	3	4	5
6	7	8	9	10	11	12
13	14	15	16	17	18	19
20	21	22	23	24	25	26
27	28	29	30	31		

November
S	M	T	W	T	F	S
					1	2
3	4	5	6	7	8	9
10	11	12	13	14	15	16
17	18	19	20	21	22	23
24	25	26	27	28	29	30

December
S	M	T	W	T	F	S
1	2	3	4	5	6	7
8	9	10	11	12	13	14
15	16	17	18	19	20	21
22	23	24	25	26	27	28
29	30	31				

2004

January
S	M	T	W	T	F	S
				1	2	3
4	5	6	7	8	9	10
11	12	13	14	15	16	17
18	19	20	21	22	23	24
25	26	27	28	29	30	31

February
S	M	T	W	T	F	S
1	2	3	4	5	6	7
8	9	10	11	12	13	14
15	16	17	18	19	20	21
22	23	24	25	26	27	28
29						

March
S	M	T	W	T	F	S
	1	2	3	4	5	6
7	8	9	10	11	12	13
14	15	16	17	18	19	20
21	22	23	24	25	26	27
28	29	30	31			

April
S	M	T	W	T	F	S
				1	2	3
4	5	6	7	8	9	10
11	12	13	14	15	16	17
18	19	20	21	22	23	24
25	26	27	28	29	30	

May
S	M	T	W	T	F	S
						1
2	3	4	5	6	7	8
9	10	11	12	13	14	15
16	17	18	19	20	21	22
23	24	25	26	27	28	29
30	31					

June
S	M	T	W	T	F	S
		1	2	3	4	5
6	7	8	9	10	11	12
13	14	15	16	17	18	19
20	21	22	23	24	25	26
27	28	29	30			

July
S	M	T	W	T	F	S
				1	2	3
4	5	6	7	8	9	10
11	12	13	14	15	16	17
18	19	20	21	22	23	24
25	26	27	28	29	30	31

August
S	M	T	W	T	F	S
1	2	3	4	5	6	7
8	9	10	11	12	13	14
15	16	17	18	19	20	21
22	23	24	25	26	27	28
29	30	31				

September
S	M	T	W	T	F	S
			1	2	3	4
5	6	7	8	9	10	11
12	13	14	15	16	17	18
19	20	21	22	23	24	25
26	27	28	29	30		

October
S	M	T	W	T	F	S
					1	2
3	4	5	6	7	8	9
10	11	12	13	14	15	16
17	18	19	20	21	22	23
24	25	26	27	28	29	30
31						

November
S	M	T	W	T	F	S
	1	2	3	4	5	6
7	8	9	10	11	12	13
14	15	16	17	18	19	20
21	22	23	24	25	26	27
28	29	30				

December
S	M	T	W	T	F	S
			1	2	3	4
5	6	7	8	9	10	11
12	13	14	15	16	17	18
19	20	21	22	23	24	25
26	27	28	29	30	31	

DON'T BE CAUGHT ABACK!
Next year has more dates and new facts

Each edition of *The Mariner's Book of Days* contains different information of interest and concern to the mariner, adding substance to an encyclopedia of fact, legend, and lore. The unique reference value of the material deserves a place on any bookshelf when the work of the calendar is done. We invite you to ensure that you receive your next copy. Send us your order for *The 2004 Mariner's Book of Days* today, and receive it in plenty of time to plan the year ahead.

Please send _____copies of *The 2004 Mariner's Book of Days* to:

Name_____

Address_____

_____

City/State/Zip_____

Price per copy is $12.95. Two or more copies are $11.00 each.
Please include $3.50 for shipping.
Maine residents please add 5% sales tax.

Mail your order to:
The WoodenBoat Store
Naskeag Road, P.O. Box 78
Brooklin, Maine 04616

Or Call Toll-Free 1-800-273-SHIP (7447)
8 A.M. – 6 P.M. EST, Monday through Friday.
VISA, MasterCard, Discover are welcome.
FAX your credit card order to 413-618-0293.
E-mail your credit card order to: wbstore@woodenboat.com
Internet: www.woodenboat.com
Payment must be in U.S. funds, payable on a U.S. bank.